Black Silver

_____

A musical

By Robert M Secreti

Writer: Robert Secreti
          bob@robertsecreti.com
          518-376-6196

Black Silver

By:

Robert M Secreti

ISBN:978-0-9777690-2-5

Circa 1870s, the taming of the Wild West

The Old West has fascinated me since childhood. Growing up, my brother and I would lay awake in our bunk beds and talk about cowboys, Indians, and settlers west. One of our favorite topics was Bass Reeves, a real western hero with 3000+ felony arrests and 14 gun fights. It wasn't until we were adults that we realized Bass was forgotten by main stream western history.

Could it be because he was larger than life? Was it because he was black? Or was it because his achievements were so monumental that they could not be written by mortal man?

In any case, Bass Reeves with the help of the Buffalo Soldiers were instrumental in the taming of the rough and tumble Old West.

My reason for developing the musical Black Silver was to try and bring to light some of the great men and women that have been lost to time. While doing this my hopes are to right a few wrongs and renew interest in who really helped tame the Western Arkansas Territory.

Enjoy Black Silver and tell your friends about it.

At this time I would to thank my wife and family for their support over the years. All the wonderful writers, and most of all my public and private teachers, especially English. Maybe I did not try as hard as I could have while in school. You have inspired me. Then again they did not have spell/grammar check in prehistoric times. If anyone feels left out remember there is a little piece of all of you in Black Silver.

Bob

LIGHTS UP ON:

COMANCHE, OKLAHOMA STREET - EVENING

> A shadow enters from stage left.
> The dimly lit town of Comanche,
> Oklahoma is in the background. The
> jingling of silver spurs can be
> heard as a figure walks toward
> center stage and addresses the
> audience.

BASS REEVES: late 30s, superhero, six foot two inches of
African American Deputy Marshal. He is a true legend of the
Western Arkansas Territory circa 1875.

                    BASS
George Reeves, a farmer politician, he owned my
daddy and he owned me.

I beat Master Reeves in a card game. Together
for three years of war I had to take flight.
With a pistol and a knife I learned to fight.

To the territories of the Seminole and Creek I
did seek.

I had quite the life with my Nellie wife.

Judge Isaac Parker sent out the call.

Five boys and five girls we had to feed.

So I happily answered his need.

Over three thousand felons we captured alive,
only fourteen dead from an injection of lead.

With thirty-two years out in the West, it was
time for a rest. No outlaw, no bandit ever beat
me. It was Bright's disease that killed Bass
Reeves.

> Bass exits the stage, the lights
> dim out. After a moment of
> silence, the sound of footsteps
> and the jingling of spurs can be
> heard. A shadowy figure appears,
> heads toward the telegraph office.
> Dance hall music begins to play
> from the local saloon. As the
> shadow nears the entrance of the
> telegraph office, the lights
> brighten.

> Three men become visible, their guns readied. The shadowy figure stops, and lights hold on the lone gunman. One of the men speaks to the figure, it's Bass.

                    MAN 1
We gotcha now, Bass.

                    MAN 2
Yeah, lawman, there's some big money out there on you.

                    MAN 3 FROM THE SHADOWS
So we ain't so stupid, are we, Bass man?

> As the figure moves closer, we see the barrel of a shotgun peeking out of the prairie duster. The figure throws back the hat and shakes out her long flowing hair. It's a woman. The hombres are startled.

> Off in another dark corner, the lights come up. A tall, lean figure is standing there with a pistol in each hand, arms crossed.

> Lights come up on the man as he walks closer, unfolding his arms. The three men have their backs turned to him. They know he's there and begin to fidget.

> Bass snickers as he speaks.

                    BASS
Yeah, we gotcha now, Bass.

> The strapping, larger-than-life figure circles, guns leveled in.

                    BASS (CONT'D)
I see you met my favorite deputy... Lily Langtry.

LILY LANGTRY: Songstress of the Prairie. Works undercover with the Ninth Cavalry Special Detachment.

                    LILY
No problem, Marshal, the sheriff is waiting.

> As Lily motions with her shotgun, she opens her coat.

> She is holding two sticks
> connected to what looks like a
> double-barrel shotgun. She is
> riding on the back of another
> person. She throws off the coat
> while jumping off.

                    LILY (CONT'D)
        Had to figure out a way to be as tall as you,
        Bass. Meet my partner, Touch Hole Kelly.

> As Bass shakes Kelly's hand, Belle
> Starr can be heard singing from
> the saloon.

> Bass walks past the telegraph
> office.

INT. SALOON

> Through the doors of the saloon,
> we see Belle swaying to the music.
> She notices Bass as she dances her
> way over and pulls him to the
> dance floor.

> Off to the side are Bat and
> Nellie, sitting cozily at a table.

> Belle and Bass continue to dance
> around the room, closing in on
> Nellie and Bat's table. Bat stares
> into Nellie's eyes as she stirs
> her drink. She smiles seductively
> at Bat. Bass and Belle round the
> last turn, and Bass glances over
> and sees Nellie again. Nellie
> giggles, gestures "yes." They get
> up and join Belle and Bass. Nellie
> makes sure she is not paying
> attention to Bass.

> They begin to rumba, moving to an
> open break.

> Belle stops and turns toward the
> audience. She pops up her derriere
> and cups her hands about her
> boobs.

BELLE STARR: a sultry saloon girl who still has a touch of
innocence. Her looks would tempt the soul of any man, then
she would steal his horse.

                         BELLE STARR (SINING)
OH, BASS MAN, YOU GONNA CATCH ME WITH MY GAMBLING ASSETS AND
THE LIGHTS OF BURLESQUE? ALL ANYONE SEES IS THESE.

                              Bass reaches for her hand and
                              holds it. He looks out to the
                              audience.

                         BASS (SINGING)
HONEY, YOU KNOW I DON'T CARE ABOUT THESE.

                              Bass lets go of Belle's hand then
                              forms his hands around his
                              breasts... smiles to the audience.

                         BASS (SINGING) (CONT'D)
IT'S NOT THE GREEN THAT MOVES ME. ALL I WANT TO SEE, NO
CRIMINALS GO FREE.

                              Bass feels his lapel.

                         BASS (SINGING) (CONT'D)
THE CASH DON'T HURT.

CHORUS: the characters that are available in the various
scenes throughout the musical.

                         CHORUS (SINGING)
IT'S NOT THE GREEN THAT MOVES ME. I'VE BEEN LOVIN IT RIGHT
ALONG. HE'S BEEN LOVIN IT.

                              As Bass and Belle sing, they look
                              at each other.

                              Belle reaches for Bass's hand, and
                              turns into his arms in a cuddle.
                              They look into each other's eyes,
                              then he sends her out.

                         BASS (SINGING)
WHEN I'M ON THE TRAIL I AIN'T HUNTIN NO TAIL.

                              Bass leads Belle into a cross
                              body, picks her up to a turning
                              basic. He then leads her into an
                              open break, to a left turn, and
                              picks her up again.

                              As Bass picks her up, his back is
                              facing the audience. Belle can be
                              seen reaching into his pocket and
                              stealing his wallet. Bass lifts
                              his left hand. As Belle turns, she
                              slides the wallet into her bodice.

> He turns her into an open break
> and lets her go. Belle dances
> offstage. Bass is left in an open
> break with his hand outstretched.
> Bat and Nellie can be seen looking
> at Bass and smiling.

> Bass turns while looking at the
> audience, slightly bewildered. He
> takes a second look at Nellie and
> Bat, then grabs a chair as he
> walks over to their table. He
> forces it between the couple.

> BASS (CONT'D)
> Well, hi ya, Bat... Set up any fixed fights
> lately? Or tricked any stupid Yankees into one
> of your poker games?

BAT MASTERSON: early 30s, broad-shouldered, barrel-chested,
sharp-dressed man. Known throughout the West as a shifty part-
time lawman, part-time gambler.

> Bat stands up, faces Bass down.
> Bass casually looks up and smiles.

> BAT
> Hey, Bass man, you calling me a cheat?

"Sheet" is used in place of the word "shit". Example:
"Sheet,man, what ya been up to?"

> BASS
> Is that all you gonna do, sheet-man. How about
> letting a tired lawman buy you and this pretty
> lady a drink?

> Bass motions to the barkeep.

> BASS (CONT'D)
> Bring us a bottle of your best chilled
> champagne and three glasses... poleze. Cuz me
> and Mr. Bat are gonna...

> Bass turns slightly, looks at
> Nellie, and reaches for her hand.
> He leads her into a rumba. The
> chorus and Bass begin to sing
> their parts.

The chorus is made up of the patrons in the saloon.

> CHORUS (SINGING)
> THEY ARE GOING TO DANCE FOREVER... OH WRONG, OH WRONG?

                              BASS (SINGING)
WHAT WOULD IT BE LIKE TO DANCE WITH THE ONE YOU LOVE?
PROMISE MY WORLD I'D WALK THE MILES,
TO DANCE WITH THE ONE I LOVE.
IF YOU EVER WERE IN LOVE, YOU'D UNDERSTAND.
SO BAD, SO BAD, TO BE IN LOVE.

                             CHORUS (SINGING)
THEY ARE GOING TO DANCE FOREVER... SO WRONG, SO WRONG?

                              BASS (SINGING)
YOU MAKE ME BLIND.
TO DANCE WITH THE ONE I LOVE.
PROMISE MY WORLD I'D WALK THE MILE, THE ONE I LOVE.
YOU MAKE MY LIFE COMPLETE.
OH OH OH THE ONE I LOVE.
TO DANCE FOREVER, THE ONE I LOVE... OH OH OH.

                             CHORUS (SINGING)
THEY ARE GOING TO DANCE FOREVER, TOGETHER... SO WRONG, SO
WRONG TO BE IN LOVE?

                              BASS (SINGING)
PROMISE MY DANCE WITH MY ONLY LOVE.
SO WRONG, SO WRONG?
THE ONE I LOVE.
TO BE THIS WAY, MY LOVE...
IF YOU EVER WERE IN LOVE, YOU'D UNDERSTAND. SO WRONG, MY
LOVE, HARD TO UNDERSTAND TO DANCE WITH MY LOVE.
INDIVISIBLE FOREVER, IN LOVE.

                                   Bass and Nellie finish their dance
                                   and they both sit down. The waiter
                                   brings their champagne and pours
                                   them a drink.

                         WAITER
              That'll be ten dollars.

                                   Bass smiles and reaches into his
                                   coat pocket. He feels around for
                                   his wallet with a stunned look on
                                   his face.

                         BASS
              My wallet... I had it before.

                                   Bat and Nellie smile.

                         BAT
              I see you met Belle Starr...

                                   Bat looks at up at the waiter and
                                   smiles.

                         BAT (CONT'D)
          I got it, Val.

                         BASS
          Belle Starr, aye... I've been looking for her.

NELLIE JENNIE: early 20s, very pretty dance hall queen. Song
writer, choreographer, and soon to be Bass Reeves' wife but
does not believe it yet.

                         NELLIE (giggles)
          Big lawman, Belle is probably halfway to
          Muskogee...

                              Bat and Nellie finish their drinks
                              and get up. Bat helps Nellie with
                              her shawl. As they leave, Nellie
                              opens up her parasol, turns, and
                              smiles back to Bass.

                              Bass is left alone at the table,
                              examining his life. His thoughts
                              are interrupted by the sound of
                              shots and yelling.

TOUCH HOLE KELLY: short, stout female acrobat entertainer.
Lily recruited her while visiting a carnival. She was the
performer who initiated antics while firing a man out of a
cannon. She is very excitable and tends to say peoples names
twice.

                              Kelly runs around Bass as she
                              talks.

                         TOUCH HOLE KELLY
          Bass... Bass Reeves, come quickly. They're
          robbing the freight office!

                              Bass jumps up, checks his guns,
                              and runs for the door.

                         BASS
          Who's robbing the office?

                              Bass and Kelly run through the
                              saloon door to the freight office.
                              Bass stops. Kelly runs through the
                              freight office door, comes back
                              out.

                              Bat leaves right behind Bass and
                              Kelly.

> With Nellie in tow holding on to
> her bonnet, they run up to the
> freight office. Bat speaks to one
> of the townsfolk.

COMANCHE, OKLAHOMA STREET

                    TOUCH HOLE KELLY
The Dozier boys. They shot old Jake
Weatherbee... Shot him dead, just missed my
head.

> Kelly goes back into the freight
> office.

The front of the freight office has a watering trough
visible. Jake's boots and legs can be seen extending from the
end of the trough.

The facade of the Comanche freight office has a period sign
on top that reads "Comanche, Oklahoma Freight Office." Horses
and riders are painted into the facade heading into the
sunset, with overstuffed saddlebags, money and dust swirling
about.

> The townspeople are milling about,
> assessing the scene.

                    BAT
The safe... is it blown?

> Touch Hole Kelly runs from the
> freight office yelling.

                    TOUCH HOLE KELLY
Sheriff Bat! Sheriff Bat! They got it all...
bonds, money, and shot Jake...

> Bat takes his hat off, rubs his
> head and eyes, then slaps his
> thigh with the hat. Bass walks
> over to Bat as they both look
> toward the freight office and
> Jake's boots. The townsfolk
> surround Bat and Bass in a
> semicircle.

                    BAT
They got it... and him.

                    BASS
What? Got what?

                    BAT
The railroad. The M-K-T, the Katy Line. The
railroad is owned through a bearer bond
corporation. Whoever holds the bonds owns the
railroad.

                              Bass turns to the audience makes a
                              face and rolls his eyes .

                    BASS
The Katy... What about the Katy?

                              Bat walks around throwing his
                              hands up in the air.

                    BAT
The Katy railroad, the money gone. This can't
be happening.

                    BASS
The money, for the Katy?

                    BAT
The money! The money... that's nothing. I am
sooo dead. The government, the Dodges, the
Kansas-Arkansas-Missouri- Texas, Railroad. The
Doziers own it now, all of it... they own the
Katy!!!

                    BASS
What do you say?

                              Bat is clearly agitated as he
                              talks.

                    BAT
The black valise that was in the safe next to
the cash contained bearer bonds. It was my
responsibility to keep them safe until next
week. Mr. Dodge from the Union Pacific Railroad
is due in to disperse ownership by order of
President Grant.

                    BASS
So you're telling me this Dodge guy doesn't own
the railroad now, Bob Dozier does. And Dodge
doesn't know it.

                              Bass takes his hat off and sits on
                              the end of the watering trough,
                              stunned.

                              Touch Hole Kelly runs through the
                              town crying the news. She stops to
                              tell a crowd of gatherers, waving
                              her arms.

                         TOUCH HOLE KELLY
          Bob Dozier killed a man. Dozier now owns the
          whole Katy railroad, because he is in
          possession of bearer bonds for the Katy.

The crowd turns and looks at each other. They begin to sing.

                         CHORUS (SINGING)
OFF WITH THE BONDS THEY WENT.
GOOD BYE TO MY KATY,
INTO THE DESERT SEA.
THEY LEFT US WITHOUT A CENT.
NOW WE CAN'T PAY THE RENT.
THEY STOLE NOT JUST THE MONEY, YOU SEE.
NO MORE JAKE WEATHERBEE.
WE HAVE TO FIND THE KATY.

                         BASS
          That's up to me to find the Katy.

                         BAT
          No, it's up to me cause they killed Jake
          Weatherbee. I have primary jurisdiction.

                         BASS
          I am the Deputy Marshal. You're the town
          sheriff.

                                   Bat fixes his coat, then
                                   straightens his tie and hat. He
                                   begins to walk off the stage. Bass
                                   sees that Nellie is left standing
                                   alone. He walks over to her.

                         BASS (CONT'D)
          Ya know, Batty, that's an excellent idea.

                                   Bass puts his arm out for Nellie
                                   to take, and they begin to walk.
                                   Bat stops cold in his tracks,
                                   raises his hand, and points at
                                   Nellie.

                         BAT
          Hey wait, she's my girl. If anyone walks her
          home, it will be me.

                         BASS
          Don't you have a murderer to catch? After all,
          you are the primary jurisdiction.

                                   Bass taps Nellie on her hand.

                         BASS (CONT'D)
          Come, Nellie, it would do me honor to escort
          you home.

                         Bass turns and smiles to Bat.

                    BASS (CONT'D)
          Bat, I'll be along shortly.

Bass smiles at Nellie, then to the audience. Nellie smiles
brightly at their antics. They walk back to the saloon.

INT. SALOON

There is nothing but commotion as men walk around talking to
each other. When Bass enters, he is surrounded by men and
dance hall girls.

                    MAN 4
          Bass, is it true whoever has possession of the
          bearer bonds owns the Katy?

                    BASS
          Don't none of you get any stupid ideas. Them
          Missouri Yankees that own the railroad ain't
          gonna let no cowpokes or dance hall queens live
          long enough to even smell them bonds. Between
          the Indians, U.S. government, and tinhorn
          gamblers, the Doziers are good as dead.

                    MAN 4
          That's good enough for me. Let's go get us a
          railroad.

                                   Man 4 raises his hand, and most of
                                   the saloon empties with him.

                                   Bass shakes his head and walks to
                                   center stage, then exits.

                                   Lily is left standing alone
                                   looking sultry, ready to
                                   entertain. She smiles out into the
                                   audience.

                                   Lily moves to mid-stage and begins
                                   a swing step. She has chorus
                                   backup.

                    LILY (SINGING)
FIFTY MILES WEST.

                    CHORUS (SINGING)
MONEY, MONEY.

                    LILY (SINGING)
WHERE DID IT GO?

                    CHORUS (SINGING)
MONEY, MONEY.

                    LILY (SINGING)
FIFTY MILES WEST. HONEY, HONEY.

                    CHORUS (SINGING)
THEY LEFT WITH MONEY.

                    LILY (SINGING)
HONEY, HONEY, BABY, BABY
GOING TO TOPEKA, MUSKOGEE.
HONEY BABY, BABY.

                    CHORUS (SINGING)
HONEY, HONEY, BABY, BABY.

                    LILY (SINGING)

WICHITA, CHINO.

                    CHORUS (SINGING)
WHERE DID THEY GO?
HONEY, HONEY, BABY, BABY.

                    LILY (SINGING)
MONEY, MONEY WILL BRING
TROUBLE, TROUBLE.
HONEY, HONEY, BABY, BABY.
FIFTY MILES WEST, BABY, BABY
TOPEKA, MUSKOGEE.

                    CHORUS (SINGING)
HONEY, HONEY,
THEY OWN THE BONDS
MONEY, MONEY, HONEY, HONEY.

                    LILY (SINGING)
MUSKOGEE, COMANCHE.
HONEY, HONEY, BABY, BABY, BABY, BABY.

                         Touch Hole Kelly runs in.

                    TOUCH HOLE KELLY
     Miss Langtry, Miss Langtry... Marshal Bass
     wants you behind the livery stable.

                         Lily exits the saloon area.

COMANCHE, OKLAHOMA STREET

The words "bearer bonds" echo through the town. Residents
congregate... with commotion.

                    MAN 1
     Bearer bonds, bearer bonds... Ya mean anyone
     can own the Katy? You just bear the bonds, show
     up in court and claim the railroad!

                              One resident, Man 5, runs off.
                              Another resident yells to the
                              leaving cowpoke.

                    MAN 6
          Hey, where you off to?

                              Man 5 stops, takes off his hat and
                              shuffles backward.

                    MAN 5
          Get my horse and supplies.

                              He turns and runs. Bat steps out
                              of the shadows. Man 5 almost runs
                              into him.

                    BAT
          Hey, haay, not so fast. You ain't a goin
          nowhere, Val Verdy. I need some more deputies,
          you're one. Now git to the jailhouse and pin on
          a star.

VAL VERDY: mid 20s,slim, light blond hair, a little weather-
beaten from living out in the desert.

                    VAL VERDY
          Aw, come on now, Sheriff. I never owned a
          railroad before.

                    BAT
          Bass is right. Them Missouri Yankee barons
          won't stop until they git their Katy back.

                              Bat steps out of Val Verdy's way.
                              Val walks away shaking his head
                              and mumbling, scuffing his feet.

                    BAT (CONT'D)
          Remember, we only got till next week. Or say
          good-bye to Comanche. Every politician in the
          country will be sticking his nose in my
          business. I spent a long time setting up in
          this place.

                              Bat looks at his watch, shakes his
                              head, and walks offstage as the
                              lights dim.

LIVERY STABLE

                              When the lights come up
                              highlighting a mural of the livery
                              stable with a paddock. As Lily
                              enters the lights brighten. Bass
                              has his boot on a crate, looking
                              toward Lily as she walks.

                              BASS
           I need you to find Sergeant Stance and ask him
           to send a squad from his Ninth Cavalry to
           twenty miles west of the dead line. I'll meet
           them in few days.

                                   Lily walks away.

                              BASS (CONT'D)
           Lily, wait.

                                        Lily stops. Bass walks up to her
                                        and gives her a hug. Bass and Lily
                                        open break, begin to sing and
                                        dance. Waltz step

                         LILY AND BASS (SINGING)

           TWENTY MILES WEST THE M K AND T.
           FROM SALINA, TOPEKA, MUSKOGEE.
           THE NINTH GUARDS ME, AND THE KATY.
           TWENTY MILES WEST,
           THEY RIDE TO BE FREE.
           WHERE THE STRONG SURVIVE.
           THEY KILL THE REST.
           THE DEAD LINE IS A PLACE IN THE WEST. FAR FROM WICHITA,
           KANSAS, AND COMANCHE.
           MY KATY AND ME.
           M, K, AND T, MY KATY AND ME.
           MARLOW, DUNCAN, MUSKOGEE,
           THE DEAD LINE SAYS IT BEST.
           THE COWARDS NEVER STARTED, AND THE WEAK WERE LEFT TO THE
           DUST.
           SALINA, TOPEKA, MUSKOGEE, A MUST OR BUST.
           TWENTY MILES WEST, THE M K AND T. MY KATY, THE TRAIN TO BE
           FREE.
           THE NINTH AND ME, MY KATY YOU SEE. THE RAIL THAT SUPPLIED THE
           WEST.
           SALINA, TOPEKA, MUSKOGEE, A MUST OR BUST.
           TWENTY MILES WEST THE M K AND T.
           THE DEAD LINE IS A PLACE IN THE WEST.
           SALINA, TOPEKA, MUSKOGEE, A MUST OR BUST.

                                        As they end their dance number,
                                        Bass's attention is focused on the
                                        commotion at the end of the livery
                                        stable. Bass leaves Lily. Bass
                                        walks to the other side of the
                                        set. The lights brighten as he
                                        walks closer. Some of the men are
                                        obscuring the outline of a well
                                        dressed lady. Nellie can be heard
                                        speaking.

                    NELLIE
I don't give kisses to strange men. Now let me
on my way.

                              Bass walks up to one of the men
                              and pulls him away, exposing
                              Nellie. From the darkness, Bat
                              emerges, stepping between the men,
                              Bass, and Nellie.

                    BASS
You boys looking for trouble?

                              Bass puts his hand on his hip. One
                              man pulls away from Bass.

                    MAN 6
I don't appreciate this Negro in a fine suit
handling me.

                              As he finishes speaking, Man 6
                              takes a swing at Bass and misses,
                              striking Bat in the gut. The blow
                              knocks Bat to his knees. Bass
                              grabs the man's hand, putting it
                              behind his back. Bat fights to get
                              up, shaking the punch off. Bat
                              struggles, then walks over to
                              Nellie and puts his arm around
                              her.

                    BAT
Bass, take him to jail. I'll be along shortly.
I want to walk Miss Nellie back to the saloon.

                    BASS
Ah ah ah... no, no, no, this is your town,
remember. I'll walk Miss Nellie back.

COMANCHE, OKLAHOMA STREET

                              Bass smiles, taps his arm. Nellie
                              smiles and holds his arm as they
                              walk away. Bat and the rowdies
                              fade to dark.

                              As they walk, Bass pushes away to
                              an open break. He then reaches for
                              Nellie's hand and walks backward
                              as he sings to a foxtrot.

                    BASS (SINGING)
WHAT WOULD YOU THINK IF I WAS FALLING IN LOVE?
IT DOES NOT MATTER THAT YOU ARE A DANCE HALL DOVE.

                              Nellie turns to an open break,
                              sings. She sways her hips to the
                              tune as Bass leads.

                    NELLIE (SINGING)
LET'S GET SOMETHING STRAIGHT, JUST A DANCE HALL GIRL I'M NOT.
I DO SING AND DANCE, AND I KNOW I AM SO, SO HOT.
AND OH, MISTER BASS, IF YOU THINK YOU GOT WHAT IT TAKES,
YOU DO NOT. I SEE YOU PRANCE THROUGH HERE ON BIG HANDSOME
RED. ALL THE GIRLS SAY YOU KNOCK THEM DEAD.

                    BASS (SINING)
HONEST, MISS SWEET NELLIE, WHEN I'M RIDING BIG RED IT AIN'T
ME, IT'S THAT WHITE SPOT ON HIS HEAD. PAY NO ATTENTION TO
WHAT IS SAID. ALL MY PRANCING DAYS A DEAD. IF YOU WOULD BE MY
DANCING DOVE.

                              Bass turns to the audience,
                              putting his hands on his heart.

                    BASS (SINGING)(CONT'D)
I SWEAR TO MISS NELLIE, I THINK I'M FALLING IN LOVE. MY
PRANCING DAYS WITH BIG RED ARE DONE. YOU ARE THE ONE.

                    NELLIE (SINGING)
YOU CALLED ME A DANCE HALL DOVE. SINGING AND DANCING IS WHAT
I LOVE. SO ALAS, MR. BASS, YOU CAN FORGET ABOUT HITTIN THIS
ASS. SO LET ME GO. I'M OFF TO THE SHOW.

                              Bass leads Nellie toward the
                              saloon door. The lights come up,
                              and there is noise and commotion.
                              Nellie stops by the door, enters
                              the saloon. She leans with one leg
                              bent and resting on the door jam.
                              Bass is left looking forlornly
                              into the saloon for a moment then
                              enters.

INT. SALOON

                              Touch Hole Kelly can be heard
                              coming by the sound of her feet.
                              She stops a distance from Bass and
                              motions for him to come excitedly.

                    TOUCH HOLE KELLY
Marshal Bass, Marshal Bass! She stole Big
Red... She rode right out of town... headed
west.

                              Lights flicker in the saloon.

                    BASS
Big Red? Who stole him!!?

                         TOUCH HOLE KELLY
            Belle Starr... Gone, her and Big Red...

                                    The patrons in the saloon begin
                                    singing and dancing. They dance
                                    around with Bass and Kelly. The
                                    two take turns dancing with the
                                    chorus.

                         CHORUS (SINGING)
GONE, GONE, GONE, HER AND BIG RED.
THERE GOES BIG RED WITH THE WHITE SPOT ON HIS HEAD.
BELLE LEAVES A PRANCING, WE ALL A DANCING,
CAUSE WE LOVE THE ROMANCING.
WITH BASS CHASING MISS NELLIE AND LOVE IN HIS HEAD.
LOVE IN HIS HEAD.
IT WAS EASY FOR BELLE TO RIDE OFF ON RED.
WHEN BASS HAS LOVE IN HIS HEAD.
WHEN BASS HAS LOVE IN HIS HEAD.
WHAT'S HE TO DO, FOR THE LOVE OF THIS LADY?
ALL HIS LIFE HAS BEEN A BIT SHADY.
WHEN BASS HAS LOVE IN HIS HEAD
FOR THIS LADY, THIS LADY.
ALL HIS LIFE HAS BEEN A BIT SHADY.
WHEN BASS HAS LOVE IN HIS HEAD.
WHAT'S THE MARSHAL TO DO,
BELLE HAS FLED WITH BIG RED?
HOW'S A HE SUPPOSE TO WIN MISS NELLIE?
WHEN HE CAN'T EVEN KEEP BIG RED.
BIG RED, GONE, GONE, GONE.
WHEN BASS HAS LOVE IN HIS HEAD.

                                    As the chorus finishes they
                                    separate sections in the saloon.
                                    Bass sings the lead here. Nellie
                                    saunters from the wall to Bass.
                                    The tempo changes here. It's still
                                    swing, just more gritty. The
                                    trumpets and horns hang on the
                                    notes in time with the "oh my, and
                                    oh why." The chorus sings back up.

                         BASS (SINGING)
OH MY, MISS NELLIE, OH MY, YOU HAVE MY HEART, OH MY, FROM THE
START.

                         NELLIE (SINGING)
OH WHY, WHAT YOU SAY? OH WHY, WHAT YOU SAY. I TOLD YOU NO, NO
WEDDING BANDS. OH WHY, OH WHY DON'T YOU GO.

                         BASS (SINGING)
OH MY, MISS NELLIE, OH MY, WORK MAKES ME SHADY. YOU ARE MY
LADY. OH MY.

                NELLIE (SINGING)
I TELL YOU NOW, MAKE NO WEDDING PLANS. I TELL YOU NOW, NO
RING, RING, NOT FOR ME. OH WHY, OH WHY, YOU AND ME, NO RING,
RING, RING, RING. WHAT TO DO WITH THAT THOUGHT.

                BASS (SINGING)
WE ARE STARS IN THE SKY. RING, RING, RING, RING FOR ME.

                NELLIE (SINGING)
I TOLD YOU NO, NO WEDDING BANDS. OH WHY, WHY DON'T YOU GO.
NO RING, RING, RING, RING. WHY DON'T YOU GO. I LOVE DANCING,
I LOVE DANCING.

                BASS (SINGING)
FIRST THINGS FIRST, FIRST THINGS FIRST. I NEED YOU IN MY
WEST.

                NELLIE (SINGING)
YOU KNOW THE REST, I LOVE DANCING, I LOVE DANCING. NOT
INTERESTED IN ROMANCING, ROMANCING.

> Nellie finishes singing walks to
> the back of the saloon and waits
> in the doorway. Bass is left
> alone. He turns toward the patrons
> of the saloon and Nellie. Then
> with a longing look, turns, faces
> the audience. Bat enters, his
> spurs clinking.

                BAT
Hold on there, big fella. You listen to me,
Nellie is my girl.

> Bass rolls his head and eyes.

                BASS
Oh, you say so? I don't think so.

> Bat moves closer to Bass. They
> stand chest to chest. Bat now
> rolls his head and eyes.

                BAT
I think so. She was with me today, not you. And
I'm going to ask her to marry me. You'll see.

> Nellie comes from the doorway,
> where she was watching the men
> banter.

                NELLIE
Hold on, you two. I am no ones girl. I am young
and pretty and a dance hall dove, not
interested in any man's love.

                    Bat and Bass turn and look at each
                    other, then to the audience. They
                    both put their hands on their hips
                    and begin to walk in a circle as
                    if stalking each other. When Bass
                    speaks, he grabs his belt buckle.
                    Bat is startled.

          BAT
Now lookie here, Bass... I love her.

          BASS
Oh yeah... I'm a gonna marry her.

                    Bat turns to the audience, arms
                    outstretched and sings. Bat and
                    Bass take turns singing. They
                    almost interrupt each other,
                    bantering, and walking. (Music:
                    foxtrot)

          BAT (SINGING)
THE TIME HAS COME FOR ME TO FALL IN LOVE.

          BASS (SINGING)
NOT WITH MY DOVE.

          BAT (SINGING)
THE FIRST TIME I EVER SAW MY SINGING DOVE, I KNEW HER BEAUTY
WAS SENT TO ME FROM ABOVE.

                    The two men turn and look at each
                    other.

          BASS AND BAT (SINGING)
THE TIME HAS COME FOR ME TO FALL IN LOVE.

                    Bass turns to the audience, sings
                    and dances around Bat.

          BASS (SINGING)
NO, IT'S TIME FOR ME TO FALL IN LOVE.

                    Bass and Bat dance around each
                    other, stopping as they sing and
                    banter.

          BAT (SINGING)
IT'S MY TIME, MY TIME TO FALL IN LOVE. HER BEAUTY WAS
SCULPTED FROM ABOVE. MY LOVELY, MY DARLING, MY SINGING DOVE.

          BASS AND BAT (SINGING)
THE TIME HAS COME FOR ME TO FALL IN LOVE.

                    Bass reaches for Bat's hand and
                    takes it into a handshake hold.

> They change sides to the beat, and
> Bass sends Bat out into an open
> break combo, letting him go. Bass
> is left standing while Bat dances
> around him.

                    BAT (SINGING)
SHE'S GOING TO BE MINE TO LOVE FOR ALL TIME. YOU'RE WASTING A
GOOD LINE. SWEET NELLIE IS MINE FOR ALL TIME.

                    BASS (SINGING)
YOU HAVE IT ALL WRONG. LISTEN TO MY SONG, AND YOU'LL BE LONG
GONE. IT'S TIME FOR ME TO LOVE MY NELLIE, MY SINGING DOVE.

                    BAT (SINGING)
YOU ARE MISTAKEN. NELLIE IS MINE FOR ALL TIME. FROM THE SHINE
OF THE MORNING SUN, TO THE BLUE OF THE EVENING MOON. WE WILL
WED SOON.

                    BASS (SINGING)
COME TO REALITY, LISTEN TO ME. NELLIE IS MY LOVE.

> There is some commotion in the
> background, causing the men to
> stop singing. The lights dim on
> Bass and Bat, come up onto action
> stage left. Two men enter running,
> and Lily follows cracking a whip.
> As the men run toward Bass and
> Bat, the lights follow.

               LILY
You hold them, Bass. They're from the Dozier
gang. I know sure as I'm standing here.

> Bat turns real quick and circles,
> looking around and trying not to
> be nervous.

               BAT
Hold on, Lily, it's not them two.

               LILY
What do you mean? I seen these varmints in
Abilene, riding with Bob Dozier.

               BAT
I said I'll take them...

> Bat steps between Bass and Lily.
> He looks at them and Bass. Val
> Verdy enters the scene.

               BAT (CONT'D)
Val, get them to the jail. Move.

                              The two men walk offstage,
                              escorted by Val. Bat follows. Bass
                              walks in a small semicircle,
                              looking at the audience then to
                              Lily.

                    BASS
          Something ain't right! I know a poker face when
          I see one.

                              As Lily speaks, she turns, points
                              to Bat, and exits with a cha-cha
                              music step.

                    LILY (OFF)
          He is up to... something.

                              Bass walks back and forth as he
                              speaks and thinks.

                    BASS
          Yeah, that's it, he's up to something. I'm
          going to have a look at Jake's body.

OUTSIDE JUDGE ROY'S OFFICE

                              The lights dim on Bass as he walks
                              toward the undertaker's office. As
                              he approaches, the lights come up
                              on the facade. A sign on the front
                              of the office reads "Judge Roy
                              Bean, Undertaker." Below that is
                              another set of words, "Part-Time
                              Justice of the Peace." Then the
                              facade raises, revealing the
                              office. As Bass enters, a portly
                              man is sitting at a desk busily
                              working. The man does not look up.
                              He acts as if Bass is not there.
                              Bass clears his throat.

JUDGE ROY'S OFFICE

                    BASS
          Excuse me, sir, I was wondering if you could
          answer a few questions?

                              The man pretends to not notice
                              him.

                    BASS (CONT'D)
          Sir, I asked you a question...

                              The man looks up, annoyed. He puts
                              his papers down.

JUDGE ROY BEAN: mid 50s, red-faced, portly, disheveled.

                    JUDGE ROY
          Yes, what do want? I'm busy.

                    BASS
          I would like to see the body.

                    JUDGE ROY
          What body?

                    BASS
          Jake Weatherbee's.

                    JUDGE ROY
          Just who the hell are you?

                    BASS
          I'm Deputy Marshal Bass Reeves.

                    JUDGE ROY
          Where's your badge? Got some identification?

                              Bass smiles and flips his lapel.
                              There is nothing there.

                    BASS
          That Belle, she got my badge too.

                    JUDGE ROY
          Well, what ya got?

                    BASS
          She stole my wallet and my badge.

                              Judge Roy pushes up from his desk,
                              stands, and walks over to Bass.

                    JUDGE ROY
          Listen, saddle tramp... You've been out in the
          desert too long. This ain't the sheriff's
          office. We do bodies here and judging. The
          sheriff gets complaints. Now get!

                              In the background, someone can be
                              seen working.

                    BASS (OFF)
          I'll be back with Bat, and you're going to show
          me what I want.

                              Bass storms off.

                    JUDGE ROY
          Kelly, Kelly! Get in here.

>   Kelly stops what she is doing and
>   the lights come up, following her.

                 TOUCH HOLE KELLY
      Yes, Judge?

                 JUDGE ROY
      Head off Bass. Go down to that Madam Fanny
      Porter's and tell her Bass is on his way.

COMANCHE, OKLAHOMA STREET

>   The lights come up, revealing a
>   well-dressed lady standing in
>   front of a house, twirling a
>   parasol.
>
>   She is walking to the beat of a
>   foxtrot, enjoying the day as Bass
>   approaches.

FANNY PORTER: Old West madam, early 40s, sultry, pretty, with
ringlets of black hair, white cheeks, and ruby-red lips. She
is an outspoken type, and is a trader of fine goods.

>   Fanny steps back to a curtsy.
>   Music blends into a cha-cha.

                 FANNY PORTER
      Oh, Mr. Bass, my name is Fanny. Fanny Porter.

>   Bass stops, looks over Fanny's
>   fanny, then looks the rest of her
>   over.

                 BASS
      Yes, I see how you got your name.

                 FANNY PORTER
      I'd like to report a situation.

                 BASS
      Looks to me like you're quite the situation...
      and under control.

                 FANNY PORTER
      Yes, on such a lovely day, a young lady wants
      the escort of a handsome man.

>   Bass shakes his head and side
>   steps. He smiles, and reaches for
>   her available hand.
>
>   Bass moves into a side step. Sings
>   to the dance beat.

                              As Bass speaks to Fanny, he taps
                              his right arm, and she folds in.
                              They begin to walk.

                              They shuffle and skip to the music
                              as they walk.

                    BASS
          You have the day right. I think you're pushing
          the "young lady" part.

                              Fanny turns and faces the
                              audience, frowns.

                    BASS (CONT'D)
          Well I'll tell you, young lady, you latch on
          right here. I'm heading to see the sheriff.

                    FANNY PORTER
          I wanted to talk to you about Bat.

                              As they walk, Bass stops dead in
                              his tracks, startled.

                    BASS
          What about Bat?

                              Fanny, using body language, slowly
                              stops, turns perpendicular to Bass
                              and addresses the audience.

                    FANNY PORTER
          We all know Comanche is a prairie rose.

                              Bass reaches for Fanny's free
                              hand. They move to an open break.

                    FANNY PORTER (CONT'D)
          I want to be Bat's rose. You want to be
          Nellie's beau...

                              As Fanny finishes, they walk to
                              the foxtrot.

                    BASS
          What about Bat?

          The music changes to a swing step. They both sing their parts

                    FANNY PORTER (SINGING)
          I'LL TELL YOU ABOUT BAT... HE'S MINE AND OH-OH SO FINE.
          ME AND BAT, WE GONNA SHINE.

                              Bass stops and rolls around Fanny
                              into an open break, facing the
                              audience.

                    BASS (SINGING)
NOW HOLD ON, JAKE IS DEAD FROM LEAD...
GONE, GONE, GONE, DEAD, DEAD, DEAD...

                              Bass steps behind Fanny. She
                              seductively shadows her bodice
                              with her fingers.

                    FANNY PORTER (SINGING)
MEN WANT LADIES BY DAY, WILD WEST TAMERS BY NIGHT.
ME, I TAME DAY AND NIGHT.

                              Fanny turns, stepping back. Bass
                              steps forward.

                    BASS (SINGING)
YOU SAW ME WITH NELLIE. I HAVE FALLEN IN LOVE.
MY LIFE FOR THE LOVE OF A DOVE.

                              Bass turns away and then back,
                              holding his heart... he stretches
                              out his arms.

The chorus is vintage 50s doo-wop style.

                    BASS (SINGING)(CONT'D)
WHAT'S THAT YOU THINK, ALL IT TOOK IS A WINK.
I'M FALLING IN LOVE.

                    CHORUS (SINGING)
FALLING IN LOVE. OH, YEAH, YEAH.

                    BASS (SINGING)
I FOUND MY LOVE, FALLING IN LOVE.

                    CHORUS (SINGING)
HE'S FALLING IN LOVE. HE FOUND HIS LOVE. OH YEAH, OH YEAH.

                    BASS (SINGING)
ALL IT TOOK WAS ONE LOOK. SHE'S ALL I EVER WANTED.

                    CHORUS (SINGING)
SHE'S ALL HE EVER WANTED. FALLING IN LOVE. FALLING IN LOVE.

                    BASS (SINGING)
SHE'S ALL I EVER WANTED. I FOUND MY LOVE.
THIS OPPORTUNITY IS MINE, I FOUND MY LOVE FOR ALL TIME.

                    CHORUS (SINGING)
FALLING IN LOVE. ALL IT TOOK WAS ONE LOOK OF LOVE.

                              Bass pushes away as if to wake up
                              from his thoughts of love.

                         BASS (SINGING)
NOW HOLD ON, JAKE IS GONE, GONE, GONE,
DEAD, DEAD, DEAD... FROM LEAD.
LET'S GO SEE THAT BAT, I'M SMELLING A RAT.

                         CHORUS (SINGING)
HE'S GOING TO BAT AND HE'S SMELLING A RAT.

                                   Bass turns and takes Fanny's hand.
                                   They turn in, then out, touching
                                   palms, then break away and turn
                                   back to back. The lights dim, come
                                   up on the facade of Bat's office.
                                   Bat is sitting out front. Bass
                                   walks through shadows. Fanny
                                   trails him, still holding his
                                   hand.

                                   Bat looks up.

                         BAT
Took you long enough.

                                   Bass looks around, then lets go of
                                   Fanny's hand.

                         BASS
You're up to something... Tell the truth, you
card-marking excuse for a lawman.

                                   Bass stomps around.

                         BASS (CONT'D)
A telegraph and some desperados are all I
stopped here for. Now I have two telegraphs:
one from President Grant, and this Dodge fella.

                                   Bass walks back and forth while
                                   speaking.

                         BASS (CONT'D)
I don't like dispatches from Yankees. Me and
the Ninth are doing just fine around here. I
want to see the body.

                         BAT
Relax, he's up to Judge Roy's.

                         BASS
My fanny... he's not up there. That's why I
brought this Fanny.

                         BASS (CONT'D)
Now get your hat and fanny moving, weez gonna
see da judge.

                                   Bat giggles, smiles.

                              BAT
Hey, where you get off saying I cheat at cards?

               BASS (CONT'D)
That's how we met. In a card game... remember.

                         Bat gets up and puts papers away
                         in his coat.

               BASS (CONT'D)
While you're in there, I want to see Jake's
death certificate.

                         Bat opens his coat, pulls out a
                         sheet of paper, and hands it to
                         Bass. He looks it over, then
                         tosses it at Bat.

               BASS (CONT'D)
What you pulling? The coroner is Doc Holiday...

                         Bass turns his head in both
                         directions, brushing off his
                         shoulders.

               BASS (CONT'D)
You see any turnips on my shoulder? He's a
dentist.

                         Bass grabs his jaw.

               BASS (CONT'D)
And not a very good one. My jaw is still sore.
Now get me up to Judge Roy Bean.

                              BAT
I can't... at least right now. Meet me up there
in an hour.

                              BASS
While on your way to straighten this out, find
that Doc Holiday. He owes me a fifty-dollar
gold piece.

                         Off lights.

JUDGE ROY'S OFFICE - LATER

                         The room is lighted with spots,
                         accenting the cast: Judge Roy,
                         Lily, Bat, Fanny, and Doc Holiday.
                         A coffin with a body dressed in a
                         Calaca (skeleton costume) is
                         tipped toward the audience. The
                         costume glows from the light.

                                        They mill about nervously, waiting
                                        for Bass. A shadow enters with the
                                        sound of spurs clinking.

                         BASS
          I want answers. What hell is that shiny thing
          in the box?

                                        Bass turns, pointing to his
                                        shoulders.

                         BASS (CONT'D)
          You see dumb, stupid written... anywhere?

                                        Music comes up to a swing step
                                        tune. Bass walks toward Fanny and
                                        looks her over. She coyly smiles
                                        at Bass and raises her hand to
                                        accept a request to dance. Bass
                                        walks by her and reaches for Miss
                                        Lily, guiding her out. The rest of
                                        the cast begins to dance.

                                        Lily steps into an open break,
                                        smiling. Bass pulls into a J hook
                                        then to a skater pose. Reaching
                                        for her hand, he stops in front of
                                        her and walks backward. He begins
                                        to sing.

                         BASS (SINGING)(CONT'D)
          SO YOU THINK OLD JAKE BEING DEAD.
          ALL DECKED OUT IN HIS CALACA CLOTHES.
          THE TOWN KNOWS THE STORY OF THE
          CALACA CLOTHES.
          THEY KNOW WHAT YOU DONE.
          NOW I COME ALONG, YOU GIVE A
          SONG. THE BONDS BEING GONE.
          ALL YOU GOT IS THEM CALACA CLOTHES.
          I'M NOT GOING AWAY. OH YEAH OH YEAH.
          WHOA THEM CLOTHES, THEM CALACA CLOTHES.
          THEY KNOW, OH YA WHOA YA.
          THEM CALACA CLOTHES.
          WHAT'S IN IT FOR YOU, AND ME, OH OH OH, NO CALACA CLOTHES.

                                        As Bass sings and dances with
                                        Lily, the Calaca starts to twitch
                                        to the tune. Fanny breaks in and
                                        sings. Lily falls back.

                         FANNY PORTER (SINGING)
          I'LL TELL YOU WHAT'S IN IT FOR YOU.

                                        Fanny rolls out and breaks hand
                                        contact, arms outstretched.

                         She reaches for Bass's lapel. She
                         rocks back and forth.

               FANNY PORTER (SINGING) (CONT'D)
I SEE YOU AIN'T WEARING NO CALACA CLOTHES.

                         Fanny steps back and turns, basic
                         step to a turning basic. Bass
                         follows.

               FANNY PORTER (SINGING)(CONT'D)
YOU BETTER STEP INTO SOME MORE MONEY, YOU NEVER MIND
THEM CALACA CLOTHES.

                         They both stop, turn, and face the
                         audience, shuffling their feet and
                         clapping.

               FANNY PORTER (SINGING)(CONT'D)
THEY MEAN MO MONEY. THEM BONDS, THEM BONDS, MO MONEY, OH OH.

                         On the last "oh, "Fanny sings it
                         louder. The calaca jumps out of
                         the coffin and dances with the
                         cast. They dance along, stomping
                         tapping, snapping fingers, singing
                         to the beat.

               CHORUS (SINGING)
THE WORLD KNOWS THEM CALACA CLOTHES.

               BASS (SINGING)
HOW LONG BEFORE THE WORLD KNOWS, THEM CALACA CLOTHES.

               FANNY PORTER (SINGING)
THINK OF YOUR NELLIE. SHE SURE DON'T WEAR NO CALACA CLOTHES.
YOU GONNA NEED MO MONEY TO KEEP THAT HONEY, MO MONEY.

               CHORUS (SINGING)
MO MONEY, MO MONEY.

               BASS (SINGING)
ALL I NEED IS MY BIG RED AND NELLIE FOR MY HONEY. YOU KEEP
THEM CALACA CLOTHES. I DON'T WANT MO MONEY, MO MONEY.

                         The chorus moves to the line of
                         dance, swinging around Bass and
                         Fanny.

               CHORUS (SINGING)
HE DON'T WANT MO MONEY, MO MONEY. HE WANTS HIS HONEY, HONEY,
BABY, BABY, OH OH OH OH.

               BASS (SINGING)
I SAY DA HELL WITH THE MONEY, I WANT TO MAKE A LIFE WITH MY
HONEY NELLIE.

                                    Bass dances to the beat. He opens
                                    his arms and hands out, stepping
                                    toward Calaca.

                        CHORUS (SINGING)
HE DON'T WANT MO MONEY, MO MONEY. HE WANTS HIS HONEY, HONEY,
BABY, BABY, OH OH OH OH.

                                    As Bass moves toward Calaca, he
                                    grabs him by the throat. The
                                    singing and dancing stop.

                        BASS
You brought me here to help you hide the bonds
that you...! Robbed? Using a dead guy as a
skeleton in a cheap suit...!

                                    Calaca breaks away from Bass and
                                    runs from him, climbing into the
                                    casket and closing the top.

                                    Bass moves to the casket and
                                    begins pounding on it.

                        BASS (CONT'D)
Get your dead butt outta there. Or that'll be
the last stupid-looking suit you will ever
wear.

                                    Calaca exits holding a teddy bear
                                    with long braids, acting like a
                                    small child being scolded.

                                    Bass looks at the cast then the
                                    audience while pulling off the
                                    calaca's hood. The cast is
                                    astonished. Lily steps forward,
                                    and speaks to the audience.

                        BASS (CONT'D)
Who da hell is this?

                        LILY
Weatherbee? The bonds. The Doziers... Oh my!

                        BASS
Now you telling me the bonds are really
missing... You best not be telling me that.

                                    Bass points to Calaca.

                        BASS (CONT'D)
So who's this?

                        LILY
This, is Everett.

EVERETT: a young, half-breed Sasquatch (Big Foot).

> Bass strokes Everett's coat.

                    BASS
He's awful hairy. Shouldn't that be his name...
Harry?

                    LILY
No... Everett is a half-breed Sasquatch.

> Bass points at Everett's feet,
> clearly agitated.

                    BASS
Where's his Big Foot? Ain't no Sasquatch with a
little foot... Look at his foot... He's got a
little foot... and what's he doing dancing out
of a coffin? Now, I want some answers.

> Everett begins to quietly move
> offstage. Bass stops him.

                    BASS (CONT'D)
Hey, Fur Boy, you wait. I have a couple more
questions.

> Everett stops and plays with his
> teddy bear.

                    LILY
I said he's half Sasquatch.

> Bass turns his head, looking
> Everett up and down, and mumbles.

                    BASS
Okay, Everett, Sasquatch, you can go, stay, or
whatever. Just don't go disappearing into the
wilderness. Don't know if a little-foot
Sasquatch can be tracked.

                    LILY
Bass, it wasn't supposed to be this way.

                    BASS
What? It looks like the whole town is trying to
fool the black guy. The bonds aren't really
missing, are they? Now, are them bonds gone or
not? And did the Sasquatch help? Who's going to
believe that a Sasquatch stole the bonds? Huh?
I'll be the laughing stock of the territory.

                    LILY
No Bass, Everett had nothing to do with the
missing bonds. He only trusts a few people. We
can get the bonds back.

                    BASS
I want statements from all of you. Don't move
an inch. Bat, let's start with you. I want
answers.

                              Bass and the cast mill about. Bass
                              removes a notebook begins and to
                              take notes. The questioning is
                              interrupted by Kelly.

                    TOUCH HOLE KELLY
Marshal Bass, Marshal Bass, come quick.

                              Bass looks toward Kelly. His back
                              is facing the audience.

                    BASS
This better be important. I got me a whole peck
of trouble now.

                    TOUCH HOLE KELLY
You better come quick. The Katy is in, and
guess who is on it.

                              Bass is wide-eyed and clearly
                              agitated by the unfolding events.
                              Now he has outsiders showing up
                              unannounced.

                              Bass turns his head back and
                              fourth, stepping sideways so the
                              audience can see his face while he
                              strains to keep his composure as
                              he talks to Kelly.

                    BASS
I am not in a guessing mood right now, Kelly!

                    TOUCH HOLE KELLY
Uh-oh, it's Jake Weatherbee and some Yankees,
Marshal. They just got off the train.

                              Bass turns and rocks back and
                              forth on his feet. Gestures to Bat
                              to come closer.

                    BASS
Bat, what you gonna do now, smart guy? The
railroad is here. You got answers? How about
you, Lily, Judge Roy? Oh, and let's not forget
Doc Holiday. What you all got...? Nothing, you
all have nothing.

                              Bass exits the stage shaking his
                              head. The lights dim behind him.

                          BASS (O.S.) (CONT'D)
     A dead Jake, and Yankees at the station. Bunch
     of amateurs.

EXT. COMANCHE TRAIN STATION

                                    The Yankees are forcing a bruised
                                    but alive Jake off the train
                                    platform.

                                    Kelly runs ahead of Bass yelling.

                    TOUCH HOLE KELLY
     I told 'im you're here. He's a coming right
     behind me.

                                    Bass's spurs can be heard, then he
                                    can be seen as the lights come up
                                    leading his way. He walks to the
                                    train platform with an entourage
                                    of saloon patrons in tow.

                                    Bass looks startled as he scans
                                    Jake.

                    BASS
     Hold on... he belongs to me.

                    BASS (CONT'D)
     Did you Yankees do this to him?

                                    Doc Holiday comes running up the
                                    ramp. He stops and looks Jake
                                    over.

DOC HOLIDAY: long, tall glass of water. Late 30s, red hair,
well-dressed dentist. Part-time desperado.

                    DOC HOLIDAY
     We ain't got no doctor, nearest one is in
     Tulsa. All you have is me. We need to get him
     to Judge Roy's now.

                    BASS
     Judge Roy? He's the undertaker. I have some
     questions for Jake. So don't knock him out with
     that laudium stuff you're always drinking.

                                    Bass turns and looks around. He
                                    points toward Judge Roy's and then
                                    to a Yankee.

                    BASS (CONT'D)
     Doc, stay away from his teeth. I want him
     talking. You Yankee, I have a few questions.
     Stay here. Now, get him up to Judge Roy.

                         BAT
Hey, I'm the sheriff here. I ask the questions
and bark orders.

                         BASS
In a pig's eye you do. We are on the railroad
platform, and I'm the Western Territory Deputy
Marshal. The railroad is my jurisdiction.
You're involved in this mess. If you are not
careful, you'll be the first one I arrest.

                              Bass points to the Yankee.

                         BASS (CONT'D)
Why is he beat up like that?

                         MAN 1
We found him on the other side of the Dead Line
left to die.

                         BASS
Did he have anything on 'im?

                         MAN 1
Nothing... just Comanches.

                         BASS
Nothing? Just Comanches, he says? Hey, come
here, boy.

                              Bass reaches for him. The other
                              Yankees look each other over and
                              shake their heads. They attempt to
                              shuffle away as a group.

                         BASS (CONT'D)
So, you good samaritans just decided to bring
him back to town... all beat up? You other
fellas stick around. I'm going to have a few
more questions for you... Doc, Bat, get him up
to the undertaker slash judge.

                              Jake is carried offstage by the
                              men. The women follow. The Yankees
                              hold back, allowing the
                              townspeople to get ahead. One of
                              the Yankees can be seen showing
                              the others a piece of paper.

                              Bass is hanging back on the
                              platform, slowly surveying the
                              scene. He turns to the audience,
                              puts his hands on his face, and
                              opens his eyes wide.

                        BASS (CONT'D)
          Comanches... Ha... seriously! Come here, you
          tadpole A hole... Yankee. Who's got them
          railroad bonds?

                              Bass reaches for a Yankee,
                              grabbing him by the side of his
                              neck. The rest scurry ahead.

                        BASS (CONT'D)
          Beat-up, near, dead Jake Weatherbee, smashed in
          the head. We're taking a walk...boy!

                              As Bass and the Yankees exit stage
                              left, only the sounds of Bass's
                              boots and the whining of the
                              Yankee can be heard.

JUDGE ROY'S OFFICE

                              Doc Holiday, Judge Roy, and the
                              Yankees are looking at Jake lying
                              on the table. Doc is working on
                              him. Bass busts through the door,
                              thrusting the Yankee by his ear on
                              top of Jake. This action pushes
                              Doc out of the way.

                              With the weight of the actor
                              pressing on Jake, he becomes
                              uncomfortable and begins to
                              twitch. Bass crinkles his face and
                              rubs his head.

                              Jake starts to twitch heavily.
                              Bass and the Yankee are forced up
                              from him. Jake jumps to his feet,
                              proclaiming he is the twitching
                              Comanche.

                        BASS
          What the...? We got us another twitching
          Comanche! Why didn't I press on to Deadwood?

                              Jake twitches around Bass, who
                              stands off to the side with his
                              coat open and hands on his hips
                              facing the audience. Jake begins
                              to sing.

                        JAKE WEATHERBEE (SINGING)
OH HOW I WISH I COULD DANCE THE TWITCHING COMANCHE.
I'M THE GUY THAT COULDN'T DANCE. JUST ANOTHER GUY.
NOW I'M THE TWITCHING COMANCHE, JAKE WEATHERBEE.
I JUST WANT TO DANCE THE TWITCHING COMANCHE.
ME AND MY FRIENDS, WE JUST WANT A STAKE IN THE WEST.
YOU OBVIOUSLY DON'T KNOW JAKE WEATHERBEE. I KNOW WHAT'S BEST.
CAUSE I'M THE DANCING MACHINE.
OH BASS REEVES, YOU STUMBLED ON THE SCHEME OF THE DANCING
MACHINE, JAKE WEATHERBEE. PLEASE HELP YOU'LL SEE, CAUSE I'M
THE DANCING MACHINE, JAKE WEATHERBEE.

                                    There is the sound of a door
                                    slamming, and the lights come up
                                    on Nellie. She walks over to them.

                        NELLIE
Okay you Comanche twins get with it. Them bonds
best be found or your butts are going to belong
to them rich Saint Louis Yankees.

                                    Nellie turns, pointing toward Jake
                                    and the Yankee.

                        NELLIE (CONT'D)
Jake, you'd be dead now if they knew where them
bonds are. You better get your memory back
fast. Bass is your only protection.

                                    Jake reaches for Bass's lapel.

                        JAKE WEATHERBEE
I'm tellin ya the Doziers got em. Who do you
think beat me up like this. They left me for
dead. Honest, Bass, we were supposed to meet
and give me the bonds back. Instead they put a
whooping on me.

                                    Bass circles around Jake, putting
                                    his hands in his pockets then
                                    taking them out. He puts his hand
                                    on his chin, rubbing, thinking.

                        BASS
You think you a hurtin now, I'm a gonna bust
your knee if I don't get a straight answer.

                                    Bass reaches for Jake. Doc Holiday
                                    gets in between them.

                        DOC HOLIDAY
Now hold on there, Bass. He's in tough shape.

                        JAKE WEATHERBEE
Yeah, I need me some water and rest. He's the
doctor.

                    BASS
          Right, a doctor. He's a flimflam man and a
          lousy poker player. And where is my fifty-
          dollar gold piece you owe me?

                              Judge Roy moves from his position
                              around to Bass.

                    JUDGE ROY
          Yes, Bass, that's a good idea. Why don't we let
          Jake rest awhile. Miss Nellie, how about taking
          the marshal for a nice little walk. You'd like
          that now, wouldn't you, Bass?

                              Bass looks at Nellie then at the
                              rest of the cast sizing up his
                              options.

                    BASS
          A walk? That would be nice. If that Jake
          disappears, you're going to see more trouble
          than you ever could have thought up.

                              Bass gives Miss Nellie his arm and
                              they exit. The lights dim on them
                              and Judge Roy's office. As the
                              couple walk out, they are
                              silhouetted on the street. Once
                              they are completely on the street,
                              the lights come up as they face
                              the audience. They begin walking
                              to the beat of a foxtrot. Bass
                              reaches for Nellie's hand that is
                              clutching his arm.

COMANCHE, OKLAHOMA STREET

                              Bass turns out. They open break
                              into a grapevine.

As Nellie and Bass dance, they speak to each other in time
with their dance moves.

                    BASS
          Miss Nellie, would I be presumptuous if I asked
          you to dance? And while we danced, could you be
          my gal? The first time I saw you I knew you
          were for me. Need I get on one knee, your love
          will set me free. All I can see is you and me.

                    NELLIE
          Now hold on you, Bass man. I'm a show girl, you
          see. No natty man on one knee is gonna woo me.
          I'm a livin my dream, singing and free. So you
          please let me be.

                                They open break, and Nellie does
                                an inside turn twice. Bass catches
                                her in a sweetheart. He drops his
                                right arm, leads her out, and
                                pulls her straight in. They clasp
                                palms and almost kiss. Nellie
                                hesitates, breaking away. They
                                both push to an outside turn. Bass
                                picks her up in closed position.

                        BASS
My Miss Nellie, oh please love me.

                        NELLIE
Mr. Bass, I told you, it's about me and free.

                                Nellie stops dancing and becomes
                                serious. They are standing side by
                                side facing the audience. The
                                lights come up on the saloon, and
                                music begins to play.

                        NELLIE (CONT'D)
You and Big Red parading through town. All the
time ladies a turning their head. Bass Reeves
the legend and his Big Red. How could you fit
me in with you and your big head and that
strapping stallion Red?

                                Nellie pushes away.

                        NELLIE (CONT'D)
The music is my cue. Time to leave.

                                Bass is left alone under a spot,
                                looking dejected with his head
                                down. Then he looks up and begins
                                snapping his finger to a Gatsby
                                swing tune. Bass groves to the
                                tune as Bat and the chorus enters
                                singing and dancing, around Bass
                                and Bat as they banter throughout
                                the song always smiling.

                                Chorus: Bat, Fanny, Calaca, Belle,
                                Lily, Doc, Kelly, Judge Roy.

                        BASS (SINGING)
NO LOVE FOR BASS AND HIS BABY. SHE'S GOT TO BE MY LADY. HER
AND ME AND A SHADE TREE.

                        CHORUS (SINGING)
NELLIE IS FOR ME. HER AND ME AND A SHADE TREE.

                    BAT (SINGING)
AH NO NO NO NO, SHE'S WITH ME UNDER MY SHADE TREE. MY NELLIE
AND ME.

                    CHORUS (SINGING)
NELLIE IS FOR ME. HER ME AND A SHADE TREE. NELLIE AND ME.

                    BASS (SINGING)
JUST HER, ME, AND A SHADE TREE.

                    CHORUS (SINGING)
JUST HER, ME, AND A SHADE TREE.

                    BAT (SINGING)
OH OH OOH NO NO NO NO, SHE'S WITH ME, AND MY SHADE TREE. MY
NELLIE AND ME.

                    BASS (SINGING)
SHE'S ONLY FOR ME, AND MY SHADE TREE. SHE'S GONNA BE MINE,
FOR ALL THE TIME.

                    BAT (SINGING)
WHY CAN'T NELLIE SEE, SHE IS FOR ME? I KNOW, I KNOW, I KNOW.

                    CHORUS
HE KNOWS, HE KNOWS, JUST NELLIE AND A SHADE TREE.

                    BASS (SINGING)
MY NELLIE FOR ALL TIME.

                    BAT (SINGING)
OH, NO NO NO, SHE'S MINE MINE MINE FOR ALL TIME. OUR LOVE
WILL SHINE.

                    CHORUS (SINGING)
OH OH OHHH, SHE'S MINE FOR ALL TIME.

                                        As Bass and Bat finish they stop
                                        singing end in an open break,
                                        looking to the saloon. Standing in
                                        the doorway is Nellie. Her hips
                                        are swaying to a rumba tune. She
                                        looks sultry and serious holding a
                                        kerchief. The cast dances to the
                                        rumba. Changing partners, as
                                        Nellie sings.

                    NELLIE (SINGING)
MY LOVE IS THE DANCE. MY ASS-ETS WON'T LAST. MY ONLY CHANCE.

                                        Still facing the audience, she
                                        snaps to her tiptoes. Her butt
                                        goes up, and she sways it back and
                                        forth. Her hands cup under her
                                        breasts.

                                        She puckers her lips while she
                                        sings, accenting her boobs and
                                        bodice.

                        NELLIE (SINGING) (CONT'D)
            I HAVE THE TWO'S.

                                        Nellie grabs her butt cheeks and
                                        swings them to the rumba beat. She
                                        seductively steps and turns, now
                                        facing the audience. She uses her
                                        hands to outline her well-
                                        proportioned body, ending at her
                                        breasts. Nellie then points to her
                                        butt, turning sideways.

                        NELLIE (SINGING) (CONT'D)
            OH...AND THESE, BOTH FOR ME AND YOU.

                                        Nellie squeezes the sides of her
                                        boobs, enhancing her cleavage.

                        NELLIE (SINGING)(CONT'D)
            WHAT'S A GIRL SUPPOSED TO DO WITH JUST TWO'S.

                                        She wipes her brow with the
                                        kerchief and tosses it away.

                                        She motions to Bat to come from
                                        the sidelines. Bat walks next to
                                        her. She reaches out for his chin.
                                        Bat leans forward until she says
                                        "thieves." He rolls his eyes and
                                        steps back into the troupe.

                        NELLIE (SINGING)(CONT'D)
            TOO MUCH DUST, TOO MUCH HEAT, TOO MANY BIG MEN, WITH TOO MANY
            DREAMS. AND TOO MANY THIEVES.

                        NELLIE (SINGING) (CONT'D)
            NOW COMES BASS REEVES, OH GEEZ.

                                        Nellie steps back, putting her
                                        hands to her lips and blowing a
                                        kiss to the audience.

                        NELLIE (SINGING) (CONT'D)
            AND THERE'S ONLY POOR LITTLE OLD ME AND THESE.

                                        She runs her hands over her
                                        breasts and bottom.

                                        The music changes to an elegant
                                        waltz.

                                   Nellie reaches for Bass, he
                                   obliges. Bass and Bat take turns
                                   trying to woo Nellie, interrupting
                                   each other. Nellie is loving it.
                                   The cast members pair up and dance
                                   the waltz. Bass and Bat pick up
                                   partners as the ladies move down
                                   the line of dance.

                      NELLIE (SINGING)(CONT'D)
NOW MARSHAL REEVES, SHOULD I DANCE OR FALL IN LOVE?

                                   Dodge enters from the freight
                                   office and stands in the doorway
                                   looking into the street.

DODGE: mid 40s jet-black hair, strong facial structure. He is
a railroad builder, civil engineer, used to getting his way.
He prides himself on his impeccable dress and ability to make
things happen. He loves women, all of them.

                      DODGE
      I'll tell you what you should be doing, finding
      my damn bonds.

                                   The dancers look up, the music
                                   fades, and they exit toward the
                                   saloon, leaving Bass and Nellie
                                   alone to face Dodge. The lights
                                   slightly dim on Dodge.

                      CHORUS
      Ah ah oh.

                                   All is quiet for a moment, then
                                   Touch Hole Kelly breaks the
                                   silence coming into the saloon.

                      TOUCH HOLE KELLY
      Marshal Bass, Marshall Bass. Dodge... Dodge is
      here with them Yankee soldiers.

                      DODGE
      That's right, squirt, Dodge is here. Who the
      hell are you?

                                   Kelly introduces herself
                                   elegantly, slightly curtsying.

                      TOUCH HOLE KELLY
      I work for Miss Langtry and Marshal Reeves. I'm
      called Touch Hole Kelly.

                                   Dodge perks up when he hears
                                   Lily's name.

                         DODGE
          Lily is here, in Comanche? Where?

                    TOUCH HOLE KELLY
          The last I knew Lily was in the here with
          Sheriff Bat.

                                        Dodge is poised.

                         DODGE
          So, we have all the players here. A conniving
          sheriff, a mistress of intrigue, a marshal that
          is a master of disguise, and my bonds are
          missing.

                                        Bass gets into Dodge's face and
                                        flicks his tie while confronting
                                        him.

                         BASS
          Now lookie here. While your Yankee butt is
          comfortable in St. Louis making money, we're
          here sweating, dealing with the riffraff your
          railroad brings in. So you had better settle
          down your Yankee butt. I'm the marshal here.

                                        Dodge looks Bass in the eye, then
                                        flicks Bass's tie, walks away, and
                                        turns.

                         DODGE
          Not for long... Get my bonds back.

                                        Dodge exits to the saloon. The
                                        lights dim.

INT. SALOON

The cast present: Dodge, Bat, Lily, Nellie, Calaca, Fanny,
Judge Roy, Val Verdy, Kelly, Doc Holiday, Belle Starr, and
townspeople.

                                        As Dodge enters saloon, the lights
                                        come up and music plays. Everyone
                                        begins to dance to a lively tune
                                        played on an upright piano and a
                                        twanging. (Kokomo in Asia Minor).
                                        Belle can be seen by the audience,
                                        but she manages to stay out of
                                        Bass's line of sight during this
                                        scene.

                                        Dodge walks through the dancing
                                        crowd to the bar, stands
                                        perpendicular to the bar facing
                                        the audience.

                    DODGE
          Whiskey, and a woman... not just any woman.

                              Dodge looks around the room at the
                              dancers.

                    DODGE (CONT'D)
          Lily!

                              Val Verdy pours him his drink.

                    VAL VERDY
          We serve whiskey and warm beer here, not women.

                              Val tries to go back to work but
                              Dodge grabs Val by his collar.

                    DODGE
          I own you, this hole of a town Comanche, and
          the Katy railroad.

                              Lily breaks from the dancers and
                              approaches Dodge. The music stops
                              as the cast circles around the
                              bar.

                              Lily gets in between Dodge and
                              Val, putting her hand on Dodge's
                              hand that is holding onto Val.

                    LILY
          Now remember, Mr. Dodge, it was your idea to
          hold the Katy's ownership in bearer bonds.

                    VAL VERDY
          Yeah, easier to swindle the land in Comanche
          from the Indians.

                    LILY
          Quote, they'll never know who to take to court.
          Just gonna play a little "hide the railroad."

                              There is the sound of a swinging
                              door slamming. Bass enters,
                              throwing tables out of the way. He
                              is holding a telegram in his hand.
                              Bass walks up to Dodge with fire
                              in his eyes. Dodge lets go of Val.

                    BASS
          What the... you're in on this too, Dodge? I
          just received a telegram from Indian Affairs.
          Apparently there is a discrepancy on where the
          Katy tracks lay.

                              Bass walks up close to the cast
                              members in the front, looking each
                              one in the eye.

                    BASS (CONT'D)
          I've spent most of my life living with the
          Indians. I speak five native languages and
          never heard one lie from an Indian.

                              Bass reaches for Dodge. He pushes
                              him to the bar, holding him by his
                              lapels.

                    BASS (CONT'D)
          Not one lie... Now I got me a whole town of
          liars, including an upstanding Yankee from St.
          Louis.

                              As Dodges speaks, he gently takes
                              Bass's hands from his lapels,
                              stands up, and straightens his
                              clothes.

                    DODGE
          Now hold on there, Marshal. I have nothing to
          do with the missing bonds. I got the right of
          way fair and square from them Indians.

                    BASS
          So why do I have this telegram then? Answer me
          that. Which lie or liars do I believe next?

                              Lily walks up to Bass and puts her
                              hand on his shoulder, trying to
                              comfort him.

                    LILY
          Take it easy, Bass.

                              Bass lifts Lily's hand from his
                              shoulder and turns his back to
                              her.

                    BASS
          You of all people, my friend Lily Langtry,
          singing goddess of the Old West, a swindler
          too.

                              Doc Holiday and Bat approach Bass.

                    DOC HOLIDAY
          Take it easy, Bass. Lily had nothing to do with
          this, honest. She knows as much as you do.

                    BAT
          Yeah, Bass, honest.

                    BASS
There, how's that? I got two "honests" from two
liars. Lily, they best be telling me the truth.

                              Elliot the sasquatch, still in his
                              calaca outfit leaves the crowd and
                              runs to Lily hugging her.

                    LILY
It's Okay Elliot, I'll be fine. The marshal and
I go way back. It's true, Bass, I walked into
this same as you... Just didn't have time to do
anything with them trail bums lookin for you.

                    BASS
How about your half-pint sidekick Touch Hole
Kelly? I suppose she knows nothing about this
either.

                    LILY
She was with me in Abilene until we met up with
you.

                              Doc gestures with his hand over
                              the top of Kelly's head and
                              snickers.

                    DOC HOLIDAY
Yeah, Bass, it went right over her head.

                    BASS
Now wee-ze getting to some truth here. Dodge,
if you swindled them Indians, I just might give
them pieces of paper to 'em. If they don't
already have them, and teach y'all a lesson.

                              Dodge walks closer to Bass,
                              invading his space. Bass steps
                              back as Dodge moves closer (chase
                              step).

                    DODGE
Wait a minute there, Marshal Bass. I'm not the
nefarious character you think I am.

                    BASS
So just who are you, Yankee...

                              Music comes up, bluesy salsa. The
                              cast opens wide into a horseshoe,
                              all dancing. Bass and Dodge, in
                              the center, begin dancing a chase
                              step. Bass chases Dodge first.

                              Dodge changes step and moves
                              toward Bass.

>   Bass steps back from the chase.
>   Dodge now leads from behind.

NOTE: In this song lyrics can be replaced with chorus or
dance steps. Nice Latin style beat possibly salsa mix.

                         DODGE (SINGING)
I'M DODGE, THE MONEY MACHINE, NEW ON THE SCENE. THE MAN WITH
THE GREEN... KANSAS CITY, ARKANSAS, GOT IT ALL, THE BELLE OF
THE BALL. THIS IS THE SONG, THIS IS THE SONG.

                         CHORUS (SINGING)
THIS IS HIS SONG. HE'S THE MAN, THE MONEY MACHINE. THIS IS
HIS SONG, THE MAN ON THE SCENE, GOT IT ALL, GOT IT ALL, ON
THE BALL, ON THE BALL.

>   Change step. Bass leads.

>   Bass and Dodge turn and move into
>   close position, begin a turning
>   basic. The timing is set so that
>   as each sings, he is facing the
>   audience, leading to an open
>   break.

                         BASS (SINGING)
YOU THINK YOU GOT THE LEAD, THE BELL OF THE BALL, THE BELL OF
THE BALL, GOT IT ALL, THE BELL OF THE BALL, THIS IS THE SONG.
I'M A LAWMAN IN LOVE.

                         CHORUS (SINGING)
THE BELLE OF THE BALL, DANCE HALL DOVE, THE MARSHAL IN LOVE.
THIS IS HIS SONG, THIS IS HIS SONG.

                         BASS (SINGING)
WITH A DANCE HALL DOVE. MY DOVE, MY DOVE. NEVER LET HER GO,
NEVER LET HER GO.

                         CHORUS (SINGING)
LAWMAN IN LOVE, LAWMAN IN LOVE. THIS IS HIS SONG, THIS IS HIS
SONG, OH YEAH, THIS IS THE SONG. NEVER LET HER GO, NEVER LET
HER GO.

>   Change step. Dodge leads.

                         DODGE (SINGING)
TEXAS, THE WEST, I WANT IT ALL... COMANCHE, DUNCAN, I'LL DO
IT WITH A GUN. ANYWHERE MY HORSE CAN RUN. I WANT IT ALL, I
WANT IT ALL.

                         CHORUS (SINGING)
THIS IS HIS SONG, DO IT WITH A GUN, HIS HORSE CAN RUN... THIS
IS HIS SONG, DO IT WITH A GUN, WHILE ON THE RUN.

Belle Starr dances with the
chorus, moving through them and
making sure the audience notices
her. She always stays behind Bass,
swaying her hips with a big smile
on her face.

Bass is now leading. They open
break. Dodge picks up the next
available partner.

BASS (SINGING)
A TERRITORY NOW, A STATE WE WILL BE. OH YEAH, THIS MY SONG.
NO YANKEE SCAM ME.

CHORUS (SINGING)
NO YANKEE SCAM ME, NO YANKEE SCAM. THIS WHAT I GOT, THIS WHAT
I GOT, FIND WHAT I GOT, FIND WHAT HE GOT, FIND WHAT HE GOT.

Lily comes from the chorus line,
turns toward the audience, and
sways her hips and sings. She
dances back into line.

LILY (SINGING)
THE NATTY MAN BASS, THIS IS WHAT HE GOT, THIS WHAT HE GOT.
SLICK AS MOONLIGHT, BASS GOT IT, BASS GOT IT.

CHORUS (SINGING)
HE GOT IT, SLICK AS MOONLIGHT, SLICK AS MOONLIGHT. BASS GOT
IT, GOT IT, OH YEAH, BASS, HE GOT IT.

DODGE (SINGING)
DOCTORS, SCHOOLS, TAXES. OH YEAH, THIS IS THE SONG.

CHORUS (SINGING)
TAXES HE IS IN, HE SINGS THE SONG. OH YEAH, HE SINGS THE
SONG. OH YEAH, HE SINGS THE SONG.

DODGE (SINGING)
FOR ME, I WANT MORE. I SING THE SONG, I SING THE SONG.
GOVERNOR YOU'LL SEE. YOU SEE, THIS IS THE SONG.

CHORUS (SINGING)
OH HE WANT MORE. THIS GUY, HE GONNA RUN. I'LL TELL YOU WHY,
THIS GUY GONNA RUN, ON A HORSE. THIS HIS SONG, THIS HIS SONG.
ON THE RUN, WITH A GUN, ON THE RUN, ON THE RUN. THIS HIS
SONG.

BASS (SINGING)
WITHOUT THEM BONDS, YOU'RE ON THE RUN.

CHORUS
CHOCTAW, CHICKASAW, WICHITA, HE ON THE RUN.

                        BASS (SINGING)
CHOCTAW, CHICKASAW, WICHITA... AND ME. YOU'RE ON THE RUN,
YOU'RE ON THE RUN.

                        CHORUS (SINGING)
DO IT WITH A HORSE, HE ON THE RUN, HE ON THE RUN. DO IT WITH
A GUN. WITHOUT THEM BONDS, HE DONE. CHOCTAW, CHICKASAW,
WICHITA, HE ON THE RUN, HE ON THE RUN.

                        BASS (SINGING)
BONDS AND ME. CHOCTAW, CHICKASAW, WICHITA.

                                    Dodge is turned and pointing to
                                    the audience.

                        DODGE (SINGING)
ME CARE, ABOUT A WHO SAW, WHAT SAW, OR CHICKASAW. I'M THE
MONEY MACHINE. I'M NOT GOING TO RUN, NOT GOING TO RUN.

                        CHORUS (SINGING)
THE MONEY MACHINE, NEW ON THE SCENE. DO IT WITH A HORSE, DO
IT WITH A GUN. HE ON THE RUN, HE ON THE RUN.
THE MONEY MACHINE, ON THE SCENE. HE SAY WHAT HE MEAN. KANSAS,
ARKANSAS, TEXAS, THE MONEY MACHINE.

                        DODGE (SINGING)
MONEY FOR ME.

                        BASS (SINGING)
WEST FOR ME. WIDE OPEN AND FREE!

                        CHORUS (SINGING)
THE MONEY MACHINE, ON THE SCENE. SAY WHAT YOU MEAN. THEY ON
THE RUN. THEY ON THE RUN. KANSAS, ARKANSAS, TEXAS,
K-A-T-E... WIDE OPEN AND FREE. WEST ON THE RUN, WEST ON THE
RUN. OH YEAH, WHY WE MUST GO... WHY MUST WE GO. THE MOON AND
THE WEST, WHY WE MUST GO. WHY WE MUST GO, TO THE STARS, OH
YEAH, THIS IS THE SONG. WHY WE MUST GO. LOOK AT WHAT I GOT,
WHY WE MUST GO. THE STARS WEST, WHY MUST WE GO. THE SONG OF
THE WEST, WHY WE MUST GO. KANSAS, ARKANSAS, WHY WE MUST GO.

                        TOUCH HOLE KELLY
        Marshal Bass, Marshal Bass, while we all were
        singing and a dancing, the Ninth Cavalry rode
        into town. Look.

                                    Lights shift toward the door. The
                                    sound of spurs can be heard.
                                    Sergeant Stance enters and reports
                                    to Bass.

SERGEANT EMANUEL STANCE: First Sergeant, ninth cavalry, U.S.
Army Medal of Honor winner in the 1870 Indian Wars. Known as
Stance.

                         STANCE
Sergeant Stance, United States Army reporting, Marshal.

                              Bass reaches for the sergeant's
                              hand, gladly shaking it.

                    BASS
Stance, good to see you. I just wired a request
to Judge Parker.

                    STANCE
As soon as the word got out about the border
and bond troubles, the Army diverted us days
ago.

                              Bass turns and looks at the cast.

                    BASS
You mean I'm not the only one suspicious of
these polecats?

                    STANCE
Apparently not, Marshal.

                    BASS
Step into my office.

                              Bass leads the way through the
                              saloon door to the street. Stance
                              follows.

COMANCHE, OKLAHOMA STREET

                              When they reach the street, Stance
                              reaches for Bass's arm.

                    STANCE
Hey, man, what the heck you got going on?

                    BASS
No kidding, Stance, we got white folks all over
that been screwed.

                              Stance has a big smile, great body
                              language.

                    STANCE
So, where's the problem...?

                    BASS
The house, Sunset Boulevard, West Coast. Your
Buffalo butt never gonna see it... Got it?

                    STANCE
Say what?

                        BASS
We got stock in the railroad too, remember.

                                        Stance has a special glow in his
                                        eyes and a half smile while he is
                                        talking to Bass.

                        STANCE
Say what... about the railroad, the Katy? It
was your idea to put the bounty money we made
into the Katy bonds.

                        BASS
I think the Chickasaw have them.

                        STANCE
Have what?

                        BASS
The bonds, our bonds.

                                        Stance has a big smile.

                        STANCE
Say what? No, they don't.

                                        Bass tries to speak, but Stance
                                        interrupts. He reaches to his
                                        pocket.

                        STANCE (CONT'D)
You think I'm going to trust some white folk
Yankees? I was the sergeant on duty the night
of the bond transfer.

                                        He taps his pocket and removes a
                                        large billfold.

                        STANCE (CONT'D)
I swapped our shares with paper. Got 'em right
here.

                                        He shuffles his feet in a little
                                        dance.

                        STANCE (CONT'D)
I'm tellin ya, got' em right here.

                                        He fans the bonds in front of
                                        Bass, smiling.

                                        Bass turns his head, putting his
                                        hands on his lapels, shocked. He
                                        leans back on his heels and rocks.

                    BASS
Us and the Chickasaw own the Katy?

                    STANCE
The Chickasaw? How do you know that?

                    BASS
Nobody dead yet. Where do you think I learned
slick as moonlight? Chickasaw. Now we have to
find them.

                              Stance points to stage left.

                    STANCE
The Mighty Ninth is right out there.

                              Lights come up on the end of the
                              main street. Enter the Mighty
                              Ninth dancing troupe in squad
                              formation.

NINTH CALVARY: Buffalo soldiers, Bass Reeves. They provide
support to aid in cleaning up the West. Very resourceful
organization. Highly respected by the Indian tribes.

                              The Ninth parade across the front,
                              snap to attention, then to parade
                              rest. There is a moment of
                              silence. A cha-cha with a real
                              nitty-gritty trumpet, horn section
                              blows. They begin to dance to the
                              song, THANKFUL.

                    NINTH CALVARY (SINGING)
AY, AY YA, AY YA, HERE WE ARE, THANKFUL. BLUE AND YELLOW,
THANKFUL. DANCING, DANCING HERE, THANKFUL, THANKFUL. TO BE
WHERE WE ARE, WHERE WE ARE. THANKFUL, THANKFUL. ROAMING THE
WEST, THANKFUL, FOR WHERE WE ARE. LIGHTED BY A STAR,
THANKFUL. TO TURN THE HEAT UP. LIGHTED BY A STAR, THANKFUL.
FOR WHERE WE ARE. THANKFUL, FOR ROAMING THE WEST. DOING THE
BEST, FOR THE WEST, THANKFUL, OF THE WEST, THANKFUL. FIND THE
TRASH, ROAMING THE WEST, AY YA. HERE WE ARE, RIDDING THE
WEST, RIDDING THE WEST, THANKFUL, FOR WHERE WE ARE. DANCING,
DANCING. HERE WE ARE THE NINTH, NATTY ON THE SCENE. HERE WE
ARE, NATTY ON THE SCENE. WE GONNA MAKE THE PLACE CLEAN. WE ON
THE SCENE. THANKFUL, AY YA. DOING THE BEST FOR THE WEST, ON
THE SCENE.

                              The chorus dances out, leaving
                              Stance and Bass standing out
                              front. They both tap to the music
                              as it fades.

                    BASS
You find them Chickasaw. Don't push'em. They'll
come to you.

                    STANCE
The Ninth is on it, boss. Hey, Boss Bass, see
you in the cactus.

                    BASS
Stance, let me hold onto them bonds. Let's keep
the Chickasaw as far from getting all the Katy
as we can. I'll put them in the bank.

                                   Bass smiles as Stance turns and
                                   hands over the wallet. Stance
                                   backs away, saluting, as the
                                   lights fade. Bass stows the
                                   billfold behind his back under his
                                   coat.

                                   The cast comes out of the saloon
                                   and surrounds Bass. They mill
                                   about, everyone talking at once.
                                   Bass pushes a way through. Belle
                                   Starr can be seen in the crowd as
                                   Bass focuses and heads toward the
                                   bank. She bumps into him from
                                   behind. Belle can be seen pinching
                                   the billfold. Bass keeps walking
                                   and gets to the front of the bank.

                                   Touch Hole Kelly comes running up.

                    TOUCH HOLE KELLY
Marshal Bass, Marshal Bass, didn't you see her?
She bumped you.

                    BASS
Who?

                    TOUCH HOLE KELLY
The lady... it was Belle.

                                   Bass immediately feels his coat
                                   and pockets.

                    BASS
Dagnabit, she got my billfold. Come on, let's
move. We got us an Indian war we have to stop.

                                   The cast mills around, then exits
                                   into the saloon. Bass is left
                                   looking perplexed in the street.
                                   He walks toward the Western Union
                                   office. In the shadows, the
                                   outline of a woman can be seen.

> She walks toward Bass. The lights
> come up. It's Belle. She fans the
> empty billfold to antagonize Bass.

                    BELLE STARR
Looking for this, Big Boy?

                    BASS
Never mind that. Where's my Red?

> Belle fans the billfold as she
> talks, seductively turning and
> swirling.

                    BELLE STARR
Don't you worry about. Handsome Big Red... he's
safe. I want to talk about the Katy.

                    BASS
What about the Katy?

                    BELLE STARR
Ever heard of Sam Starr?

                    BASS
You know I have. I'm the one who arrested him
for cattle rustling and freight robbery.

                    BELLE STARR
Sam Starr is getting out of jail, and you're
going to help him.

                    BASS
No way, Belle. He's a robber and a hustler,
serving three years in Provo.

> Belle walks around Bass, smiling.
> Bass circles, not letting her out
> of his sight.

                    BELLE STARR
What if a resourceful girl had proof Sam was
framed for the robbery. He was with me all
day... and night. We were holed up in a little
cabin just off the Choctaw Creek.

                    BASS
He's a crook and you know it.

                    BELLE STARR
No, Bass, he is a cattle rustler who was trying
to feed his people. He don't belong in no
Provo.

                         BASS
You stole my wallet, then my horse. Now you
think you're in a bargaining position.

                         Belle gets close to Bass, looking
                         fine in his space.

                    BELLE STARR
Big Red and your wallet are out behind the
livery stable. Them bonds of yours, let's just
say they ain't too far from them Chickasaw.

                    BASS
Okay, girl, you got my attention.

                    BELLE STARR
On our way up to Choctaw Creek, we stopped and
visited a man. Looked something like that Mr.
Dodge fella. Sam made me wait up on the ridge.

                    BASS
Dodge? You sure. He's robbing his own freight
offices?

                    BELLE STARR
I'm not saying that. I'm just following the
money.

                    BASS
We never did find that freight cash on Sam. He
sure wasn't talking.

                         Bass turns and walks back and
                         forth. Grabs his lapels.

                    BASS (CONT'D)
Your Sam Starr ain't gonna see the light of day
unless I get them bonds back, all of 'em.

                         Belle turns and points toward the
                         side of the livery. She pats
                         Bass's arm as she rests her hand
                         in the crook. Bass escorts Belle
                         offstage.

                    BELLE STARR
Come on, Marshal, we have a big red horse to
visit.

                         Bat and Judge Roy exit from the
                         saloon. They talk as they walk to
                         center stage, stop.

                    JUDGE ROY
I told you it was taking a big chance letting
them bonds out of our sight.

                         BAT
Look, I know the Chickasaw have them. So does
Bass. You can bet he has Stance and the Ninth
out looking for them Indians.

                         JUDGE ROY
Chickasaw can only be found if they want to.
You and Dodge better get a looking and make a
deal.

                         BAT
Dodge? They'll kill him. He swindled them out
of their land.

                         JUDGE ROY
That's your problem, and your idea started
this. Blame it on the surveyors. Make peace
with the Indians or we're all dead, including
this town.

                              They part ways. Two female figures
                              walk from the darkness of the
                              stage spinning parasols.

                         FANNY PORTER
I just can't believe it. Bass Reeves is in love
with you and you want nothing to do with him.

                              Nellie stops and steps back,
                              closes her parasol. She uses both
                              hands to point to her figure.

                         Nellie
Look at this body... look. How long do you
think this will last with a strapping gent
around like Bass? I'd be a cow with saggy boobs
and a child on each knee.

                         FANNY PORTER
I see where that Bat Masterson headed. I'll
take my chances with saggy boobs and a child on
my knee.

                              Fanny turns and looks back. She
                              shakes her butt and smiles while
                              walking offstage.

                         FANNY PORTER (CONT'D)
Maybe two.

                              Nellie walks in a half circle,
                              placing her hands on her hips then
                              turns to face the audience. Begins
                              to sing SAGGY BOOBS to a banjo-
                              picking tune.

                         NELLIE (SINGING)
MARRIAGE IN THE 70S WHAT WOULD IT BRING. SAGGY BOOBS FOR ME
AND A HOUSE FULL OF OFFSPRING.
NOT BORN WITH MUCH, I PLAN TO KEEP WHAT I GOT.
MARRIAGE IN THE 70S IS NOT WHAT I WANT.
ALL A GIRL CAN DO IS SING IN A HALL, OR STAY HOME AND LOOK AT
A WALL.
SAGGY BOOBS IN THE 70S, NOT RIGHT FOR ME.
IT'S LIKE BEING WHIPPED THEN TIED TO A TREE.
WHEN I DANCE, WHEN I SING, WHO ME NEED A RING?
SAGGY BOOBS IN THE 70S, THEY'RE NOT FOR ME.
TO HAVE SOMEONE TO LOVE, DOES THAT SOUND LIKE FUN? PICKING UP
AFTER A MAN! THAT MAKES ME WANT TO RUN.
MY CLOTHES AND MY CUP, THEY ARE MINE WHEN I GET UP.
AT TIMES THEY'RE ALL RIGHT, MEN AND THEIR STUFF. AFTER I HAVE
MY WAY, ENOUGH IS ENOUGH.
TODAY FOR ME, A KID ON EACH KNEE. THAT'S NOT WHAT I SEE. FOR
THAT BASS AND ME.
MARRIAGE IN THE 70S, WHAT WOULD IT BRING?
SAGGY BOOBS AND A KID ON MY KNEE.
HERE IN THE WEST A GAL IS FREE. MARRIAGE IN THE 70S, WHAT?
WHO ME? TODAY IN MY LIFE, BECOME SOME MAN'S WIFE. NOT ME
SAGGY BOOBS IN THE 70S, IN LOVE WITH A MAN,
I'LL SAVE US A LIFE OF WEDDED MISERY. I'M JUST GOING TO SING.
THEY COME TO COMANCHE WITH THEIR SHINY GOLD DUST. SOME TO
LOOK AND SOME TO LUST. ME, GETTING MY SHARE, WELL THAT'S A
MUST. THIS NELLIE GIRL HERE IS NOT GOING TO RUST.

                              Nellie stops singing and looks in
                              two different directions as if she
                              is confused. Her thoughts are
                              interrupted by Bat.

                    BAT
Nellie, Nellie, finally... I have something to
say to you.

                              Bat dramatically puts his hand on
                              his heart.

                    BAT (CONT'D)
Nellie, I love you, I love you, and want you to
be my wife.

                              Nellie turns her head back and
                              forth, looks. She shakes her head
                              slightly and throws her arms up in
                              the air.

                    NELLIE
What! What is it with you jackass-type western
men?

                              Nellie puts her hands on her hips.

                         NELLIE (CONT'D)
You think us women are going to fall for every
saddle tramp in a suit that offers us a
proposal. I certainty am not. Now get your
derby headed butt outta here and find them
bonds.

                              Nellie turns and walks away. She
                              can be heard mumbling to herself
                              as she exits. The lights dim
                              behind her.

                    NELLIE (O.S.) (CONT'D)
All this action going on, nobody gonna be
listening to me sing.

INT. SALOON

                              Fanny Porter is seated, waiting.
                              Nellie enters.

                    FANNY PORTER
Man troubles, honey? I specialize in man
troubles.

                    NELLIE
Oh no, Fanny. Mine's just singing.

                    FANNY PORTER
If I help you sing, you help me with my man
problems?

                    NELLIE
You, man problems? You got it all going on,
honey. They pay you, leave knowing you don't
love'em. My crowd, they think I love them all.

                    FANNY PORTER
It's Bat...

                    NELLIE
Now wait a minute. I want nothing from that Bat
mastering of nothing. He tips good and loves my
singing.

                    FANNY PORTER
You mean you don't love Bat!

                    NELLIE
Honey, I don't love nothing. Singing, dancing,
champagne, bed by nine... ish. Keep them gold
pieces coming.

                    FANNY PORTER
So, you will help me?

                              Nellie looks a bit confused.

                    NELLIE
What's wrong with you, girl? All gushy over a
man?

               FANNY PORTER (GIGGLES)
Times are changing. Getting harder to keep a
clean house.

                         Fanny giggles.

               FANNY PORTER (CONT'D)
I think I can corral Bat. A handsome man with a
gun. I think I can...

                    NELLIE
You got more faith in mankind than I do. You
just keep him tipping, and liking my music.

                              Nellie smiles. They both get up,
                              arm in arm, and look back at the
                              audience, they smile as they exit
                              together.

JUDGE ROY'S OFFICE

                              Val Verdy, Bat, and Doc are
                              sitting or standing around Roy's
                              desk.

                    JUDGE ROY
Okay, bright guys. We don't get them bonds back
from the Indians, we have no town.

                    VAL VERDY
Real easy, huh Doc? Jake got a whooping, Bass
is here.

                              Their discussion is interrupted by
                              the sound of a door slamming open.
                              Lily enters.

                    LILY
I'm gonna be kicking some butt around here.
Bass thinks I'm involved with you polecats.
You're suppling me with an escort as far as
Wichita. I'm hooking up with the Ninth.

                    VAL VERDY
How do you know they're there?

                    LILY
I don't. They'll find me. We leave at seven
a.m.

                    JUDGE ROY
Lily, we can't get you an escort for tomorrow.

                    LILY
Your chuck wagon, cook, four extra horses, and
a goat. I like fresh drinks.

                    JUDGE ROY
My cook? He's working in the hotel. We're
booked.

                    LILY
Doc can cook. Just make sure he washes his
hands, and no dental work while cooking. My
wagon will be at the back door six a.m. for
supplies. Your cook and chuck wagon better be
waiting.

                              Judge Roy smiles while talking,
                              then puts his hands on his heart.

                    JUDGE ROY
Aw Lily, anything for you. You know that.

                    LILY
I should have known better. You're the one that
gave me the tip on them outlaws.

                    JUDGE ROY
Lily, I have a business to run. It costs money
to patrol the territory and operate the Jersey,
Lily.

                    LILY
I have to go. I'm packing after my seven
o'clock show.

                    JUDGE ROY
Lily, I love ya.

                    LILY
Is it me, or the money in your hotel?

                              Judge Roy smiles. Lily exits.

                    BAT
I have all my resources looking and listening.
The Chickasaw claim they don't have them.

                    JUDGE ROY
What! They don't have them?

                    BAT
No, Judge. The Indians have them, we think.

                    JUDGE ROY
Who's we?

                    BAT
The Chickasaw.

                    JUDGE ROY.
This is getting complicated. The Indians say
they don't have them. You're not making any
sense. They are the Indians.

                    BAT
No, Judge, the other Indians.

                              Judge Roy leans back on his chair
                              and puts his hands on both sides
                              of his head.

                    JUDGE ROY
More dang Indians.

                    BAT
This was Indian land. There may be something to
their claim to the land west of the Katy and
parts of the Katy.

                    JUDGE ROY
Nice easy PR job. Mystery of the lost bonds.
What a newspaper headline. Stores, shops, full.
My hotel, busting at the seams. Dime novels,
all gone to which Indian tribe controls the
railroad.

                              Roy gets up by pushing himself
                              from the desk in mid-sentence. He
                              shakes his finger as he says
                              "that's crap."

                    JUDGE ROY (CONT'D)
That's crap, that's crap. Dat ain't right. What
are we going to do all day, without a town? You
numbskulls.

                              Again their meeting is interrupted
                              by the sound of a door slamming
                              open. Dodge enters.

                    DODGE
Yeah, that's right. It's Dodge, owner of the
railroad. You guys have your fingers all over
this. Fill me in, or the railroad will never
stop in Comanche again. After Duncan it will
veer west, then south. Got it?

                              They all get up and speak
                              together.

                     VAL, ROY, DOC, AND BAT
Mister Dodge, please, we'll get the bonds back
and clear up the title issue with the Indians.

                     DODGE
There is not a title issue. Dodge don't cheat,
not even the natives on a reservation... got
it?

                     VAL VERDY
How are your fares doing? A ticket to Comanche,
anyone? Ten dollars. How's them ten dollars
doing there, Mr. Dodge?

                     JUDGE ROY
He's right, Dodge. The frog skins are rolling
in.

                     DODGE
Frog skins?

                     JUDGE ROY
Yankee greenbacks.

                     BAT
The Indians call 'em frog skins. No concept of
paper money. The promised pile that swims away.
That's what they call it.

                     DODGE
You mean to tell me the Indians don't know what
to do with the bonds?

                     VAL VERDY
Not that simple. They know the paper means
something to us.

                     DODGE
Val is right. Something bigger is going on
around here.

                     JUDGE ROY
We have been had! By who?

                     DODGE
It appears someone a lot smarter than you
oatmeal heads.

                     JUDGE ROY
Mr. Dodge, listen, calm down. We have our best
people working on this.

                              Dodge takes Roy's lapels in his
                              hands. The others move in closer
                              to them, showing concern that
                              Dodge may get violent.

                         DODGE
Listen to me, you furry-faced panhandle rodent!
I want my railroad back. I expect my railroad
back.

                                   He lets go of Roy's lapels, then
                                   gently strokes them to straighten
                                   them out.

                         DODGE (CONT'D)
You certainly have put Comanche on the map. Now
get the Katy back in my pocket.

                                   Dodge exits. The men nervously
                                   look at each other.

                         DOC HOLIDAY
Oatmeal heads... I resent that.

                         VAL VERDY
We all must have been sucking on that bottle of
laudium you use to get involved in this scheme.

                         DOC HOLIDAY
Hey, I have consumption.

                         VAL VERDY
Yeah sure... consumption of cigars, loose
women, booze, and all-night card games.

                                   Doc moves toward Val.

                         DOC HOLIDAY
They're beautiful women. Who like to have fun.
Loose... You ever seen the laces on them
corsets?

                                   Doc raises both hands and
                                   shudders.

                         JUDGE ROY
Now hold on, fellas. Bickering ain't gonna get
us the Katy back. Doc, you get to the hotel and
start a poker game in the saloon. Val Verdy,
you hang out in the background listening to
rumors. Start some if you have too. Get them
carpetbagger Yankees talking. Bat, you come
with me. We are going to find us a smart
Indian.

                                   They all exit the stage.

INT. SALOON

                                   Doc is sitting at the table
                                   dealing cards with Judge Roy.

                              He's surrounded by town residents.
                              Doc cuts cards with a man that has
                              his back to the audience. Touch
                              Hole Kelly sees the man.

                    TOUCH HOLE KELLY
          Doc, Doc, you nuts, crazy? Bass finds out that
          lobo outlaw is here, we're all going to be in
          front of Judge Parker.

                    DOC HOLIDAY
          Say hello to the Apache Kid.

                    TOUCH HOLE KELLY
          I know who he is.

                              Doc is talking to the Kid.

                    DOC HOLIDAY
          Tell Touch Hole Kelly here what you told me.

          APACHE KID: late 30s, ebony black hair. Well-known
          highwayman. Suspected of a few murders, many robberies.

                    APACHE KID
          Lily Langtry and the Ninth are closing in on
          the bonds. Just west of Walters Temple.

                              Judge Roy interrupts the
                              discussion by clearing his throat.

                    JUDGE ROY
          Hold on, wait. Before you all get your dander
          up. I got enough problems with Bass right now.
          Kid, get outta here.

                    APACHE KID
          I want my money.

                    JUDGE ROY
          Money?

                    DOC HOLIDAY
          I promised the Kid one thousand in gold and a
          full pardon in Texas from you. When he tells us
          where the bonds are.

                              Roy puts his hand through his hair
                              and pulls on his beard.

                    JUDGE ROY
          No, five hundred now, then five hundred when
          the bonds are here.
                    (MORE)

                    JUDGE ROY (CONT'D)
          I don't even know why I'm doing this. Lily will
          be on them bonds anytime now.

                         DOC HOLIDAY
          He says no. They're too late. Whoever has the
          bonds keeps them moving. He says he'll send a
          runner here with the next destination.

                                   Roy motions to the barkeep. He
                                   brings over a box. Roy hands the
                                   Kid a bag of coins.

                                   The Kid lets out an Apache yell as
                                   he exits.

                         APACHE KID
          Aye ya-aye ye!

                         JUDGE ROY
          A thousand bucks for a railroad... hmm.

                         DOC HOLIDAY
          Five hundred, Judge. I hated to do it. We have
          to get the word out. We have to pay good money
          for information.

                         JUDGE ROY
          Try starting out a little lower next time.
          Judge Parker's reach is getting into my
          jurisdiction. A pardon?

                         DOC HOLIDAY
          The Kid is in desperate need of money for a
          lawyer. He's on Bass's to-do list.

                         JUDGE ROY
          What makes you think he won't run off to Mexico
          with my full pardon and the five hundred?

                                   Roy runs his hands through his
                                   hair then his beard, pulling on
                                   the tip.

                         DOC HOLIDAY
          All the better. If he's smart, he'll stay in
          Mexico and keep his mouth shut.

                         JUDGE ROY
          One thing for sure. I'm on Bass Reeves to-do
          list now, and I want off.

                                   Roy turns to the cast, speaks.

                    JUDGE ROY (CONT'D)
          Okay, folks, according to the Apache Kid, Lily
          and the Ninth are closing in on them bonds.
                         (MORE)

                    JUDGE ROY (CONT'D)
So we all might as well hunker down and watch
the show. The next drink is on me.

                         The upright piano twangs, glasses
                         clank. Judge Roy walks over and up
                         onto the stage in the saloon.
                         Everyone stops and listens. The
                         piano quiets down.

                    JUDGE ROY (CONT'D)
Now, folks, I would like to introduce the
latest addition to the Jersey Lily Saloon. Our
bevy of entertainment... the crown of Comanche.
The one and only "Doves of Distinction."
Singing backup and dancing with Nellie. This
little number is also choreographed by our
lovely Nellie. Let's hear it for Nellie and her
Doves.

                         Triple time swing song here with
                         gritty snare drum and clarinet,
                         speakeasy Gatsby sound. Nellie is
                         centered, with her dancers around
                         her. As the music comes up she
                         taps and sways a bit to get the
                         feel. Nellie interacts with the
                         chorus.

                    NELLIE (SINGING)
IT'S A PARTY NIGHT, GOT MY LIPSTICK RIGHT.

                    CHORUS (SINGING)
DA DOO DO DA DA, PARTY NIGHT.

                    NELLIE (SINGING)
LIPSTICK RIGHT, IT'S A PARTY NIGHT.

                    CHORUS (SINGING)
LIPSTICK RIGHT, PARTY NIGHT.

                    NELLIE (SINGING)
DRESS SO TIGHT, JUST ONE MORE NIGHT.

                    CHORUS (SINGING)
PARTY NIGHT, LIPSTICK RIGHT, PARTY NIGHT,
DRESS SO TIGHT, GO DADDY GO.

                    NELLIE (SINGING)
DON'T WANT TO LOVE, JUST PARTY TONIGHT, TO DANCE WITH THE
FACES, PARTY NIGHT.

                    CHORUS (SINGING)
DA DA DOO, DO TA DA, PARTY TONIGHT, WE WE TEE TEE.

                        NELLIE AND CHORUS (SINGING)
DANCE WITH THE FACES, A THOUSAND FACES. JUST WANT TO SWING,
SWING, TONIGHT, TONIGHT. I'M THE DANCING DOVE, JUST PARTY, NO
LOVE TONIGHT.

                           CHORUS (SINGING)
DO DA TA, TA DOO DO, JUST PARTY TONIGHT, NO LOVE IN SIGHT.

                           NELLIE (SINGING)
I'M IN PARADISE, WHEN I DANCE AT NIGHT, MAYBE YOU'LL BE MINE,
TO DANCE TONIGHT.

                         NELLIE AND CHORUS
DANCE WITH, DO BE, DANCE NIGHT, DANCE WITH ME, DO BE, DO BE.
DANCE NIGHT, DANCE NIGHT, SWING NIGHT, SWING, SWING NIGHT.

                              NELLIE
NEVER GOING TO SLEEP AGAIN, SWING NIGHT, PARTY NIGHT, DANCE
NIGHT.

                    NELLIE AND CHORUS (SINGING)
DO BE DO, TA DA, TA DA DA DA, CHOO CHOO CHOO.

                              NELLIE
DRESS TIGHT, LIPSTICK RIGHT, PARADISE TONIGHT, PARTY NIGHT.
DANCE UNTIL DAYLIGHT, BRIGHT LIGHTS, PARTY NIGHT, JUST ONE
MORE, PARTY NIGHT. SO DANCE WITH ME, ONE MORE NIGHT. BRIGHT
LIGHTS, PARTY NIGHT.

                    NELLIE AND CHORUS (SINGING)
DO BE DO DA DA DA TA TA TA.

                           NELLIE (SINGING)
DON'T STOP, SWING NIGHT, NO TIME FOR LOVE, DON'T STOP, SWING
NIGHT.

                           CHORUS (SINGING)
DO BE DOO TA TA DO... BE DO, TA TA.

                           NELLIE (SINGING)
I'M IN PARADISE, WHEN I DANCE AT NIGHT. MAYBE YOU'LL BE MINE,
DANCE TONIGHT, DANCE NIGHT, DANCE NIGHT.

                           CHORUS (SINGING)
DO BE DOO, TA TA DO, BE DO, TA TA. DANCE NIGHT, MINE TONIGHT,
DANCE NIGHT.

                           NELLIE (SINGING)
NEVER GOING TO SLEEP AGAIN. SWING NIGHT, PARTY NIGHT.

                           CHORUS (SINGING)
DO BE DOO, TA TA TA DO, DO BE DO, TA TA DO. DRESS TIGHT,
LIPSTICK RIGHT, DANCE TONIGHT, PARTY NIGHT, BRIGHT LIGHTS.

                    NELLIE (SINGING)
DANCE TILL LIGHT, PARTY NIGHT, BRIGHT LIGHTS, DANCE NIGHT,
MAKING LOVE WITH MY DANCE TONIGHT, PARTY NIGHT.

                  NELLIE AND CHORUS
DO BE DO DA LA LA DA DA. BRIGHT LIGHTS, PARTY NIGHT, DANCE
TONIGHT, DREAMS OF LIGHT, PARTY NIGHT, DANCE TONIGHT.

                        NELLIE
I'M A STAR TONIGHT, WHEN I DANCE AT NIGHT. BRIGHT LIGHTS,
DANCE TONIGHT, SWING SWING, DANCE DANCE, PARTY TONIGHT.

              NELLIE (SINGING) (CONT'D)
IT'S A PARTY NIGHT, GOT MY LIPSTICK RIGHT.

                  CHORUS (SINGING)
DA DOO DO DA DA, PARTY NIGHT.

                  NELLIE (SINGING)
LIPSTICK RIGHT, IT'S A PARTY NIGHT.

                  CHORUS (SINGING)
LIPSTICK RIGHT, PARTY NIGHT.

                  NELLIE (SINGING)
DRESS SO TIGHT, JUST ONE MORE NIGHT.

                  CHORUS (SINGING)
PARTY NIGHT, LIPSTICK RIGHT, PARTY NIGHT,
DRESS SO TIGHT, GO DADDY GO.

                  NELLIE (SINGING)
DON'T WANT TO LOVE, JUST PARTY NIGHT, TO DANCE WITH THE
FACES, FACES, PARTY NIGHT.

                  CHORUS (SINGING)
DA DA DOO, DO TA DA. PARTY TONIGHT, WE WE, TEE TEE.

              NELLIE AND CHORUS (SINGING)
DANCE WITH THE FACES, A THOUSAND FACES. JUST WANT TO SWING,
SWING, TONIGHT, TONIGHT, I'M THE DANCING DOVE, JUST PARTY, NO
LOVE TONIGHT.

                  CHORUS (SINGING)
DO DA TA, TA DOO DO. JUST PARTY TONIGHT, NO LOVE IN SIGHT.

                  NELLIE (SINGING)
DON'T WANT TO LOVE, JUST PARTY NIGHT, TO DANCE WITH THE
FACES, FACES, PARTY NIGHT, PARTY NIGHT. WHEN I GO OUT I JUST
WANT TO DANCE. OH, DRESS SO TIGHT, JUST RIGHT FOR TONIGHT. OH
OH, WO, OH.

                              Nellie finishes with a smile. She
                              and the chorus exits the stage.

                              The lights dim, then come up on
                              Judge Roy, Doc Holiday, and Bat
                              seated at a table.

                              Foot steps can be heard, it's
                              Kelly. She burst through the
                              saloon doors.

                    TOUCH HOLE KELLY
          She's here, She's here, and on her way!

                    JUDGE ROY
          Who?

                    TOUCH HOLE KELLY
          Lily Langtry and the Ninth, and she don't look
          happy.

                              Activity with mumbling and
                              excitement in the saloon. Lily
                              enters through the door, clearly
                              agitated, walking heavily. Spence
                              follows. She stops and puts her
                              hands on her hips.

                    LILY LANGTRY
          Where is that conniving Bass Reeves?

                              Dodge enters and walks back and
                              fourth.

                    DODGE
          That's what I want to know.

                              Bass enters.

                    BASS
          There are a few things I want to know. Val
          Verdy, arrest Dodge.

                              He points to Dodge. The saloon
                              patrons gasp. Val walks over to
                              Dodge puts a cuff on him.

                    DODGE
          You can't arrest me. You got nothing on me.

                              Bass takes a second look at Dodge.

                    BASS
          Conspiracy to defraud the Indians, stealing
          from your own railroad. Filing a false report
          to a peace officer. Do you want me to keep
          going? While you're at it, Val, you may as well
          arrest the whole dang town for conspiracy. You
          all are in on it.

                    VAL VERDY
        Marshal, we can't arrest the whole town. It's
        never been done.

                    BASS
        They said what I've been doing out in these
        parts couldn't be done either. Three thousand
        felony arrests, fifteen desperados dead. I
        think I can handle a town of amateurs.

                    LILY LANGTRY
        Before you go arresting anybody, I got a bone
        to pick with you, Bass. Who do you think you
        are, sending us out on a wild-goose chase into
        the Dead Line? You knew where them bonds were
        all the time.

                    BASS
        Yeah, I got wind of their cochamamie scheme
        right from the beginning. Sorry Stance, I had
        to play dumb and send you into the wilderness.
        Now let's get to business.

                                Bass turns and points to the stage
                                door. Belle and Sam Starr walk on
                                stage together. She has her hand
                                in the crock of Sam's arm.

        SAM STARR: Old West, notorious highway man married to Belle
        Starr.

                    BASS (CONT'D)
        Belle, come in here, bring Sam. You see, until
        I had a private talk with Miss Belle, we had no
        idea that our Mr. Dodge was orchestrating his
        own robberies with Sam Starr. Sam, is this
        true?

                                Sam nods yes.

                    BASS (CONT'D)
        There are a few problems that can be fixed, Mr.
        Dodge. Sam is free because he is willing to
        tell us the business deal between you, him and
        the robberies. Suppose we don't want to know?
        Suppose the freight company gets their lost
        money back with that carpetbag of yours filled
        with cash and bonds? Hey Apache Kid, bring it
        out.

                                Apache Kid enters from the stage
                                door carrying the bag.

                    BASS (CONT'D)
        See now, the Kid here has been the owner of
        your railroad all the time.
                        (MORE)

                         BASS (CONT'D)
          But the Apache Kid don't want it. He wants a
          pardon. The government wants happy Indians, and
          they're not happy. You get what we're about to
          agree to, Mr. Dodge?

                         DODGE
          Well, you know at our last board meeting we did
          discuss the local's claim to some of the land
          west of the dead line. I believe we can work
          out a settlement.

                         BASS
          That "some of the land" you're referring to
          better be the some they want. Got it?

                              There is the sound of a chair
                              being thrown. Calaca's mothers
                              enters.

          MA-MA SASQUATCH: mother of Everett, the dancing calaca. She
          is a half-human, sensuously beautiful creature with slender
          legs and flowing hair.

                         MA-MA SASQUATCH
          Where is that Marshal Bass? My son Everett
          didn't come home for dinner.

                              Everett walks from the back of the
                              stage to the beat of a Gatsby
                              swing tune. The cast swings and
                              sings with Everett.

                         EVERETT (SINGING)
          HERE I AM, MAMA. SORRY I DIDN'T MAKE IT HOME FOR DINNER,
          'CAUSE I'M EVERETT THE SASQUATCHING, DANCING MACHINE.
          OH YEAH, OH OH YEAH.

                         CHORUS (SINGING)
          OH YEAH, OH OH YEAH.

                         EVERETT (SINGING)
          MY DADDY WAS A FARMING MACHINE. HE SAW, HE SAW, MY MAMA ALL
          HAIRY AND LEAN, THE WALKING MACHINE.

                         CHORUS (SINGING)
          OH OH YEAH, OH OH YEAH.

                         EVERETT (SINGING)
          WITH EACH STEP, EACH STEP, SHE TOOK, HE WOULD SAY, TAKE
          ANOTHER STEP, TAKE, TAKE ANOTHER STEP. MY HEART, REACH REACH
          OUT, TAKE A STEP, TAKE A STEP. SWING AND JIVE, SWING AND
          JIVE.

                      CHORUS(SINGING)
SWING AND JIVE, SWING AND JIVE, TAKE A STEP, TAKE A STEP.
SWING AND JIVE.

                      EVERETT (SINGING)
THEIR EYES MET, THEIR EYES MET, MAMA KNEW SHE COULD LOVE THAT
FARMING MACHINE. THAT'S HOW I BECAME EVERETT THE DANCING
MACHINE. FROM THE KING OF JIVE, AND QUEEN OF SWING, BIDDLE BE
BOP.

                      CHORUS (SINGING)
FROM THE KING OF JIVE, BIDDLE BE BOP.

                      EVERETT (SINGING)
HEY MAMA, I'M THE DANCING MACHINE. NOW THAT STORY IS LEGEND
OF MY MAMA AND THE FARMING MACHINE. THAT QUEEN OF SWING, AND
THE KING OF JIVE.

                      CHORUS (SINGING)
THAT QUEEN OF SWING, AND THE KING OF JIVE.
BIDDLE DEE BE, BIDDLE DE BOP, BIDDLE BE BOP, BOP, BOP, BOP.
THE QUEEN OF SWING, AND THE KING OF JIVE.

                      EVERETT (SINGING)
IT WAS HARD TO STAY ALIVE. THE TOWN DID NOT LIKE THEIR JIVE.
WE HAD TO HIDE TO STAY ALIVE. IF IT WASN'T FOR SWING AND
JIVE, SWING AND JIVE.

                      CHORUS (SINGING)
SWING AND JIVE, SWING AND JIVE. SWING AND JIVE, SWING AND
JIVE.

                      EVERETT (SINGING)
THE LOOK IN THEIR EYE, I WOULDN'T BE ALIVE, FOR THE SWING AND
JIVE, SWING AND JIVE.
BIDDLE DEE BE, BIDDLE BE BOP, BOP.

                      CHORUS (SINGING)
JIVE, SWING AND JIVE.
BIDDLE DEE BE, BIDDLE BE BOP, BOP.

                      EVERETT (SINGING)
THEIR EYES MET, EYES MET, MAMA KNEW SHE COULD LOVE THAT
FARMING MACHINE.
DADDY KNEW WITH EACH STEP, EACH STEP, THERE WAS SOMETHING IN
THE AIR. HE SAID, HI LOVE, HI LOVE. I LIKE YOUR STEP, COME
JIVE WITH ME, JIVE WITH ME.

                      CHORUS (SINGING)
HE SAID, HI LOVE, HI LOVE. I LIKE YOUR STEP, COME JIVE WITH
ME, JIVE WITH ME. JIVE, JIVE, WITH ME.

                      EVERETT (SINGING)
I'M YOUR BIG JIVE DADDY, HI LOVE, HI LOVE, I'M YOUR BIG JIVE
DADDY. THERE'S SOMETHING IN THE AIR. AND SHE SAID, MY LOVE,
MY LOVE. I ALWAYS WANTED A BIG JIVE DADDY, JIVE DADDY.

                    CHORUS (SINGING)
HI LOVE, HI LOVE, HI LOVE, HI LOVE. COME JIVE WITH ME, JIVE
WITH ME.

                    EVERETT (SINGING)
NOW THAT STORY IS LEGEND OF MY MAMA AND THE FARMING MACHINE.
THAT QUEEN OF SWING, AND THE BIG JIVE DADDY
BIDDLE DEE BE, BIDDLE BE BOP.

After Everett and the cast finish the Big Jive Daddy song and   *
dance, Stance and the Ninth enter center stage. The music
comes up with a samba mix for the remainder of this ending
scene. The cast gets a dance number and or lyrics as they
parade across center stage. The rest of them sing and dance
to the tunes in the background.

                    STANCE (SINGING)
EVERYBODY IS OUT FOR SOMETHING, AND YOURS.

                    CHORUS (SINGING)
AND YOURS, FORTUNES IN THE WIND.

                    STANCE (SINGING)
THEY SEE THEIR FORTUNES IN THE WIND.

                    CHORUS (SINGING)
THE NEXT TO TRY TO TOUCH THE SKY.

                    STANCE(SINGING)
ENOUGH FOR ALL.

                    CHORUS (SINGING)
NO NEED TO LIE.

                    STANCE (SINGING)
THE DESERT AND THE SKY, THEY BELONG TO NO ONE. EVERYBODY
COMING SHOWING UP FOR NOTHING.

                    CHORUS (SINGING)
EVERYBODY COMING, NO NEED TO LIE.

                    STANCE (SINGING)
LIFE'S WORTH MORE THAN NOTHING, THAN NOTHING. WE, A WE. THE
NEXT TO TRY, THEY SEE THEIR FORTUNES ON THE WIND.

                              Exit the Ninth. Enter Fanny and
                              Bat.

                    FANNY PORTER (SINGING)
EVERYBODY DESERVES A FRIEND. I CAN MAKE HIM FEEL ALIVE. I CAN
HOLD HIM TONIGHT.

                    BAT (SINGING)
EVERYBODY WANTS LOVE TONIGHT.

                    FANNY PORTER (SINGING)
I CAN MAKE HIM FEEL ALIVE TONIGHT.

                    BAT (SINGING)
I CAN MAKE YOU FEEL ALIVE TONIGHT. I DON'T MIND BEING ALIVE
TONIGHT, ALIVE, ALIVE.

                    FANNY PORTER (SINGING)
ALIVE, ALIVE. ALIVE, ALIVE.

                    BAT (SINGING)
NOT SURE ABOUT TOMORROW, ALIVE TONIGHT, CHECK IT OUT. NOT
SURE ABOUT TOMORROW. UNO LOVE TONIGHT.

                    FANNY PORTER
ONE LOVE TONIGHT.

                    BAT (SINGING)
WHERE OH, WHERE OH, I'D LIKE TO SEE YOU MOVE TONIGHT.
SOMETIME I'M LONELY, OH NO, OH NO. I'D LIKE THE MOVE TONIGHT,
OH NO OH NO.

                              Fanny winks, and while flipping up
                              her skirt, she smiles.

                    FANNY PORTER (SINGING)
I THINK I'M IN LOVE TONIGHT.

                              BELLE AND SAM STARR DANCE TOGETHER
                              AS THEY CROSS THE STAGE.

                    BELLE STARR (SINGING)
AYE YA OH, I FOUND MY LOVE AGAIN, AGAIN.

                              They dance seductively around each
                              other, smiling as they gaze into
                              each other's eyes.

                    SAM STARR (SINGING)
AYE YA, BELLE, FREED NOW, HI YA, FREE, DESERT FREE.

                    BELLE STARR (SINGING)
I FOUND MY LOVE AGAIN. GOOD AGAIN, LOVE AGAIN.

                    SAM STARR(SINGING)
GOOD AGAIN, FREE AGAIN, NOTHING LIKE LOVE AGAIN. LIKE LOVE.

                              In this part of the scene, Lily
                              and Doc are in line. The samba
                              step picks up speed. Their voices
                              are tuned into sound like they are
                              singing through a voice cone.
                              Example: using equalizer changing
                              frequency response.

                         DOC HOLIDAY (SINGING)
A POKER GAME, A CUTE LITTLE GIRL TO ROCK. A POKER GAME, A
CUTE LITTLE GIRL TO ROCK.

                         LILY LANGTRY (SINGING)
THE DESERT SKY, GOLDEN ON THE STAGE, MAKE ME ROCK. AYE YA
WHY, AYE YA WHY? GOLD MAKES ME LOCO. THE STAGE AND THE SKY.

                         DOC HOLIDAY (SINGING)
A POKER GAME, AND A CUTE LITTLE GIRL, MAKES ME LOCO. GOLD
MAKES ME ROCK.

                              Roy and Kelly samba out across the
                              stage. Everett and Mama samba
                              through with Val Verdy and the
                              Apache Kid.

BASS AND NELLIE RUMBA OUT, BIG SMILES, INSIDE TURNS, OUTSIDE
TURNS. THE MUSIC CHANGES TO A GRITTY SALSA WITH THE CAST
DANCING INTO A CHORUS LINE. THEY ALL TAKE THEIR BOWS.

                                             LIGHTS DOWN.

                         THE END